Called to Follow

A Daily Devotional and Small Group

Discipleship Resource

Going Deeper
— A Journey with Jesus —

Volume 3

John D. Herman

Rambling Star

An imprint of Blue Grande Publishing

Published by Rambling Star Publishing

Mechanicsville, VA

USA

Cover Design by Heather Heckel

Cover Art Copyright Luciany | Dreamstime.com

Series Logo Art Copyright Twindesigner | Dreamstime.com

Scripture quotations are taken from the New Revised Standard Version

© 1989 Division of Christian Education of the National Council of Churches of Christ

in the United States of America. Used by permission. All rights reserved.

Also by John D. Herman

Going Deeper: A Journey with Jesus

Yearning for God

God Comes to Us

The Fruit of the Spirit

The Body of Christ

Acknowledgments

I GIVE THANKS… for your partnership in the gospel. This study guide has developed over several years of walking the faith together with the people of Peace Lutheran Church in Charlottesville, Virginia. We thank God for the deeper journey into which God has led us. I am especially grateful to the members of the Discipleship Team (Jenny Cudahy, Tom Czelusta, Deb Meyers, Dave Poole, Ruth Poole, and Nancy Schmitz) who have worked together with deep devotion to fulfill the dream of creating our own discipleship curriculum. Thanks also to Jean Eckert-Dobbs, Dave Poole, and Ruth Poole for providing helpful feedback for the revision of this third book of the series. My thanks also to the devotional writers, whose names appear in this volume, and who have graciously permitted the use of their reflections. I'm very grateful to Heather Heckel, whose decision to publish this series in a variety of formats will make it easily available to others on the journey. Finally, I thank my wife Leslie, who has lovingly and patiently supported me, and who is walking with me into a new life direction. *The peace of Christ be with you always* — John Herman.

Contents

Prologue

Going Deeper: A Journey with Jesus

How this Series Came to Be

OVER THE YEARS, at conferences and workshops where we leaders of Peace Lutheran Church have led presentations about congregational spiritual growth and discipleship groups, we have been asked why we don't create our own discipleship curriculum. The answer is simple. The task has seemed overwhelming if not impossible. Where would we start? How would we do it? How could we come up with the people-hours necessary to write and produce such a resource? Besides, although not all of our participants were enthusiastically supportive of Greg Ogden's *Discipleship Essentials*, it still was the best discipleship workbook we could find (and could we actually improve upon that?).

Somewhere along the way (in other words, through the guidance of the Holy Spirit) we came up with an approach, and then a plan. What if we designed five worship and adult education series for 2011, so that they would provide the foundational material for our own discipleship curriculum? And that is what we did. We planned worship and education series (*Yearning for God; Who is This God We Believe In?; Come to the Water; Life on the Vine; The Body of Christ*), and asked congregational members to write daily devotions to accompany each series. Much of the material in this series is based on sermons, course content, and devotions from these worship series in 2011. As you read the chapters, you will notice names of people (members of Peace Lutheran Church, Charlottesville, VA) who wrote particular devotions to accompany the original worship series. When no name appears, the section was written by the author, John Herman.

How to Use this Resource

This discipleship series is intended for use by small groups and individuals, for people new to the faith as well as those who have grown up in the church. Although written by a Lutheran pastor for a Lutheran congregation, the resource invites a wider mainline Christian audience. The series is designed to promote daily quiet time dedicated to being in the Word, study, and prayer, spiritual disciplines that promote the work of the Holy Spirit in your life. There are six days of readings in each chapter. You will get more out of it when you read and reflect daily rather than trying to cover an entire week in one or two sessions.

You will also get more out of it by using this resource together in a small group of 3-6 people. I am convinced that faith grows best in the context of small groups. That is, we are more likely to be growing spiritually when walking together with other disciples. Making disciples involves developing significant Christ-centered relationships, and that happen in small groups.

Small groups will want to use the final chapter section: *Taking It Further: Small Group and Chapter Summary Questions*, as a starting point for their weekly discussions. Begin together with a review of Chapter Ten (Small Group Guidelines), and decide about a small group covenant. Further suggestions and strategy for using this series can be found in *Chapter Ten: Next Steps*. The other books of the series can be found at your favorite online bookstore in ebook and print formats.

Why I Believe in Small Groups

After thirty years of pastoral ministry, I've come to the conclusion that a small group ministry is essential for churches that want to grow disciples. They are not just an add-on for those people who might be interested in them. Following the pattern of the early church in Acts 2:42-47, small groups should be an essential structure of the church.

It is my hope that you will use this resource with a small group of 2-5 other people. Consider these essential benefits brought about by small groups. Small groups using this resource will:

- help grow Christians deeper in Jesus Christ;
- encourage the daily spiritual disciplines of Bible reading, prayer, and meditation;
- connect people to each other and build close relationships;

And not only that, but small groups can also help to foster a culture of discipleship within congregations. Small groups:

- help a congregation move toward more authentic relationships. Churches usually remain on the level of casual acquaintance without them.
- help to foster honesty and transparency in congregational relationships;
- broaden the care ministry of the congregation;
- change people…and changed people change congregations.

Introduction to *Called to Follow*

This is the third book of the series, *Going Deeper: A Journey with Jesus*. It is a "self-contained" study guide about our response of discipleship to Jesus' invitation to follow him. By self-contained, I mean that you do not have to read books one or two before taking up this book. In book one (*Yearning for God*), we see how encountering Jesus Christ transforms us. In book two (*God Comes to Us*), we address the big questions: who is God and who are we? These questions invite us into a journey to know the God who is Father, Son, and Holy Spirit, the God of grace who creates, redeems, and sustains us, and who invites us into a lifelong relationship.

In this third book, we will focus on the invitation of Jesus Christ to come to the water (of baptism) and the call to all people to follow him as his disciples. We will make use of the "baptismal covenant" as the framework for our study. The baptismal covenant, used in the *Affirmation of Baptism* service in the hymnal, *Evangelical Lutheran Worship*, is a series of five promises that summarize what it means to follow Jesus Christ. The chapters of this book, *Called to Follow*, focus on the promises of the baptismal covenant, one phrase at a time. By the way, Methodists, Episcopalians, and Presbyterians (and probably other Christians) also refer to the Baptismal Covenant and the Affirmation of Baptism.

I hope that this book will be a helpful companion for a wide variety of people: for new Christians, for youth and adults in confirmation classes, for new church members (for example, in a Pastor's Class), and for many long-time Christians who want to go deeper in their understanding of what it means to be a follower of Jesus Christ. May you be led to know the Living Water that quenches your deep thirst, and in knowing him, may your life never be the same.

Theological Foundation

Discipleship to Jesus Christ means learning to follow Jesus. Learning to live the way of Jesus. Learning to live by the Spirit. My more technical definition is: discipleship to Jesus Christ is "the intentional, communal, lifelong journey of being conformed to Jesus Christ through the power of the Holy Spirit to accomplish God's purpose in the world."[1] In other words, discipleship is at the same time an invitation, a gift, God's transforming work, and our life response to that invitation, gift, and transforming work.

The risk of writing a discipleship curriculum over five volumes is that the theological foundation is also spread across the volumes. In other words, the theology taught in volume two is often assumed in volume three. For example, in book two, the Christian faith is described as a "down religion," meaning that there is nothing we can do to make our way to God; God comes to us.

Looking at the table of contents for this volume (the life commitments of the Baptismal Covenant), one might assume that we are placing the emphasis on the Christian life as something that we do. But that is not our intent. This is not a manual on how to be a good Christian. It is not a "to do" list about how to be a disciple. Discipleship is our response to God's grace and the call of Jesus Christ to follow him in a lifelong journey. It is the role of the Holy Spirit to bring people to faith in Jesus Christ. Being joined to the death and resurrection of Christ, we are set free to live a new life in him. In book four, we focus on the Spirit's work of growing the character of Christ (the fruit of the Spirit) in disciples of Christ, so that by the renewal of their minds and hearts, they may increasingly seek to serve God and God's kingdom.

Discipleship is not some content or information that is learned, as much as it is a way of life that is lived in a community of faith. Discipleship is an enculturation process, and the faith practices (or the life commitments of the Baptismal Covenant) are the ways we learn to live out our faith. The faith practices are modeled and taught not so that disciples might become more spiritual or holy. Rather, disciples live this life so that they may open themselves to God's work and become more effective for God's use in God's world. The Holy Spirit uses the faith practices to draw us to God, to shape and form us, to nurture us in faith, to conform us to Christ, and to align us to the pursuit of God's will and God's kingdom.

Chapter One: Come to the Water

DISCIPLESHIP IS OUR RESPONSE to God's grace and God's call. It is the living out of the covenant of our baptism. The *Evangelical Lutheran Worship* hymnal provides a service of *Affirmation of Baptism* for various occasions: for individuals and congregations to renew or reaffirm their baptisms; for people being confirmed in the faith; for the reception of new members, and for times of transition in the lives of people.[2]

Imagine yourself in a church on Pentecost Sunday as seven young people stand up in front of the congregation and profess their Christian faith. They say that whereas their parents spoke for them some years ago, now they are speaking for themselves. They affirm their baptism and say that they intend to live as disciples of Jesus. And all the worshipers are also invited to reaffirm their own baptisms.

> *Pastor: "You have made public profession of your faith. Do you intend to continue in the covenant God made with you in holy baptism:*
> *to live among God's faithful people,*
> *to hear the word of God and share in the Lord's supper,*
> *to proclaim the good news of God in Christ through word and deed,*
> *to serve all people, following the example of Jesus,*
> *and to strive for justice and peace in all the earth?"*
>
> *Those affirming their baptism: "I do and I ask God to help and guide me."*

We call these five promises our part of the "baptismal covenant" with God. Together they provide a thorough description of the life our baptism calls us to live in the world, (the Christian vocation). They are a helpful summary of the life of a disciple of Jesus.

Together they describe the recurring rhythm of being nurtured by God's gifts for God's mission in the world. There is an essential rhythm of inward and outward, (coming and going, gathering and scattering, or inhaling and exhaling): inhaling (living among the people of God and hearing the Word and sharing the supper) and exhaling (demonstrating the good news in words and deeds, serving others in the example of Jesus, and working for justice and peace).

Finally, the response of the disciple, "I do, and I ask God to help and guide me," acknowledges the reliance upon God's gracious Spirit in shaping disciples, forming the church, calling them into God's mission, and strengthening them for God's mission.

In the chapters that follow, we will focus on all of the statements of the baptismal covenant, one phrase at a time.

Prayer of Thanksgiving for Baptism[3]

We give you thanks, O God, for in the beginning your Spirit moved over the waters and by your Word you created the world, calling forth life in which you took delight. Through the waters of the flood you delivered Noah and his family. Through the sea you led your people Israel from slavery into freedom. At the river your Son was baptized by John and anointed with the Holy Spirit. By water and your Word you claim us as daughters and sons, making us heirs of your promise and servants of all. We praise you for the gift of water that sustains life, and above all we praise you for the gift of new life in Jesus Christ. Shower us with your Spirit, and renew our lives with your forgiveness, grace, and love. To you be given honor and praise through Jesus Christ our Lord in the unity of the Holy Spirit, now and forever. Amen.

Day 1: Baptism

> **Ezekiel 36:25-26** *I will sprinkle clean water upon you, and you shall be clean from all your uncleannesses, and from all your idols I will cleanse you. ²⁶ A new heart I will give you, and a new spirit I will put within you; and I will remove from your body the heart of stone and give you a heart of flesh.*
>
> **Ephesians 2:8-9** *For by grace you have been saved through faith, and this is not your own doing; it is the gift of God-- not the result of works, so that no one may boast.*

On March 9, 1980, in Prince of Peace Lutheran Church in Princeton, New Jersey, Leslie and I brought forward our firstborn child to be baptized. "We present Kristin Nicole Herman to receive the Sacrament of Holy Baptism." For that special day, Leslie had purchased a long baptism dress for Kristin. A dress which looked to me to be a few sizes too big, because when we put it on her, the dress hung several inches below her feet. But Leslie assured me that it was the correct size, and that those kinds of garments were supposed to hang below her little feet.

I didn't think more about it, until the day before her baptism. I got a call from our pastor, who wanted to know just one thing. "Was Kristin's dress the kind which was very long?"

"Yes," I responded.

"Did it hang below her feet several inches?"

"Yes, that's the style," I assured him, now more confident that we had purchased the appropriate garment.

"OK, thanks," he said. "I'll see you tomorrow in church."

The next day we were among the worshipers in the sanctuary when it came time for the baptism. We brought Kristin to the font. Pastor Schott began the baptism liturgy by speaking about Kristin's dress. He said that at this point in her life, the dress appeared to be too big for her. But soon she would grow into it, and it would fit her.

Baptism is like this, he said. At this point in Kristin's life, she is unaware of what is happening to her. But as she grows up, and as her parents share their Christian faith with her, as she is nurtured in the faith and receives the gifts of God, she will grow into her baptism. Her whole life will be a journey into living out her baptism.

For those of us who were baptized as babies, there comes a time or times later in our lives when we affirm what happened to us in our baptism. Over the next several days and weeks, we will be discussing what this "affirmation of baptism" means.

Questions for reflection:

Have you been baptized? If so, where and when did it happen? How old were you? Did you have sponsors? What have you heard or what do you remember about your own baptism?

If you have not been baptized, what questions about baptism do you have?

What might be the advantages and disadvantages of being baptized as a baby, as compared to a child or an adult?

What do you think grace (Ephesians 2:8-9) has to do with baptism?

As you think about your own baptism, pray the *Prayer of Thanksgiving for Baptism* **(on page 6).**

Day 2: Remembering Baptism

> **2 Timothy 1:3-7** *I am grateful to God-- whom I worship with a clear conscience, as my ancestors did-- when I remember you constantly in my prayers night and day. [4] Recalling your tears, I long to see you so that I may be filled with joy. [5] I am reminded of your sincere faith, a faith that lived first in your grandmother Lois and your mother Eunice and now, I am sure, lives in you. [6] For this reason I remind you to rekindle the gift of God that is within you through the laying on of my hands; [7] for God did not give us a spirit of cowardice, but rather a spirit of power and of love and of self-discipline.*

When many of us were baptized, we were just babies. We were not aware of what was happening to us. Our baptism was a gift from God; nothing that we deserved or earned; nothing that we requested or expected. It was a gift. Over the years we have unwrapped the gift and tried it on and claimed it as our own.

Many of us have grown up in the Christian faith and have come to understand what God has done for us in Jesus Christ. We know that God loves us. The faith that we were given has become our own. We have learned about the message of the Bible and the meaning of our faith. We have been nurtured in the faith through the help of parents, grandparents, relatives, friends, teachers, pastors, youth group leaders so that we would come to know God as our own God. All this has happened so that the seed of faith that was planted in us might grow into our own faith.

That was the hope of our parents and sponsors when they presented us at the baptismal font. That was the hope of the gathered assembly when water was poured over our heads and we were marked with the cross of Jesus Christ. That was the hope of parents and sponsors when they promised to raise us in the faith. That someday we would come to say "Yes" to what God has done for us in our baptism. That we would say "Yes" to the Christian faith. And that we would say "Yes" to Jesus Christ, profess our faith in Jesus Christ as our Lord, and promise to live as his disciple.

How are we to "remember" something we cannot actually remember (since most of us were baptized as babies)? Remembering in this sense means to deepen our appreciation for what Jesus has done for us. How can we do that? Observing the baptismal font as we enter and leave the sanctuary is one way to remember our baptism. We may even dip our fingers in the water and retrace the cross of Christ on our foreheads. Another way to remember our baptism is to participate with the congregation in the baptism of another person, and agree to support and pray for that person in his or her new life in Christ. We can also recommit to the promises made at our baptism or our confirmation by regularly affirming our baptism.

Questions for reflection:

Do you know your baptism anniversary? How do you "remember" your baptism?

What does (your) baptism mean to you?

Prayer: *Thank you, Lord, for calling me to the waters of baptism. Thank you for the transforming work of your Spirit and the gift of your love and forgiveness. Thank you for all the people who have helped to raise me in the faith, especially for particular grandparents and parents or others who modeled the life of discipleship for me and with me. Amen.*

Day 3: God's Promises and Ours

> ***Matthew 3:13-17***   *Then Jesus came from Galilee to John at the Jordan, to be baptized by him. [14] John would have prevented him, saying, "I need to be baptized by you, and do you come to me?" [15] But Jesus answered him, "Let it be so now; for it is proper for us in this way to fulfill all righteousness." Then he consented. [16] And when Jesus had been baptized, just as he came up from the water, suddenly the heavens were opened to him and he saw the Spirit of God descending like a dove and alighting on him. [17] And a voice from heaven said, "This is my Son, the Beloved, with whom I am well pleased."*

Think of all the gifts we receive in baptism. Consider the promises of God that come to us. In baptism we are joined to Jesus Christ, to his death and resurrection. We are forgiven. We enter into God's covenant people: the worldwide community of faith as well as a local Christian church. As with the baptism of Jesus, we believe that we receive the Holy Spirit in baptism, and marked with the cross of Christ, we are claimed as God's own children: we belong to Jesus Christ.

Not only do we receive God's promise that God will be our God, and that we are God's children, in baptism we also make some of our own promises. If we were baptized as small children or infants, our parents and baptismal sponsors made these promises for us. And as we have grown up in the faith, and grown into our baptism, we have come to affirm these promises. Just as God promises to be our God, we also promise to live as God's people. Our baptism calls us to become ministers (or servants, or disciples) of Jesus Christ. We are filled with the gifts of the Holy Spirit to offer our lives in loving service to God and to our neighbor.

When young children are baptized, their parents speak for them. The parents (and sponsors) take on the responsibilities to help their children grow in the Christian faith and life. They promise: to raise their children within a Christian community, to teach them the Lord's Prayer, to place in their hands the Bible, and to nurture them in faith and prayer so that: their children may learn to love and trust God, proclaim Christ through their words and actions, care for others and the world God has made, and work for justice and peace.[4]

And we the congregation promise to support and pray for them in their new life in Christ. Why? Because it takes a community to raise a disciple.

Live today with the reminder that you are walking wet: washed in the water, marked with the cross of Jesus Christ and gifted by the Spirit to live for God in all you do. (As you shower or wash your hair, allow the water pouring over your head to remind you of your baptism.)

Questions for reflection:

How is the baptism of Jesus similar or different from your own baptism?

Choose one of the promises of God received in baptism (mentioned above). Write a prayer of thanks for this promise.

Day 4: Baptism Changed My Life

> ***Acts 8:35-38*** *Then Philip began to speak, and starting with this scripture, he proclaimed to him the good news about Jesus.* *[36] As they were going along the road, they came to some water; and the eunuch said, "Look, here is water! What is to prevent me from being baptized?"* *[37]* *[38] He commanded the chariot to stop, and both of them, Philip and the eunuch, went down into the water, and Philip baptized him.*

Jerri Haussler, a writer and homemaker, wrote an article several years ago for the *Lutheran* magazine entitled, "Baptism Changed My life." It was the baptisms of her children that changed her life and led her to reaffirm her own baptism.

Neither Jerri nor her husband were active in a church. To get their parents off their backs, they had their 4 year old daughter and 3 month old son baptized. She writes: "Because of the vows we took, something happened to me—something that neither I nor the pastor who baptized our children would have predicted. In less than six months, I had enrolled in a new-member class at our neighborhood Lutheran congregation in Lincoln, Nebraska."

Several years later, Jerri relates that the family worships together regularly, and she has participated in a Bethel Bible series as a student and then as a teacher. She has taught Sunday School and Vacation Bible School. She has even served as a congregational leader.

Because of her children's baptisms, her life has changed. She finds herself much more loving, caring, and willing to give. She thinks about others more often than she did before this experience of baptism: "my work through my congregation and my efforts for the sake of others grow out of my faith. I do these things because of my love for God. I cite them only to show the wonder of God's persistent Spirit in bringing me to renewed vitality within the church and among God's people. As surprising as it was to me, and likely to many others, the fact is that my faith was renewed through the baptism of my children. Great things began to happen in my life. Because I was an inactive member, some people and pastors might have thought that I didn't deserve to have my children baptized. But I am grateful to God that the pastor did not say 'no' when we came to have our children baptized. Baptism not only made a difference for my children, it also changed my life."

In what may appear to be merely the splashing of water and the saying of words, we enter a greater reality than before. God enters a life and changes it. You may not remember anything about your own baptism. You may not know the date. You may no longer have the certificate. But having received the Holy Spirit and having been claimed as one of God's children, there is no telling what God may have in store for you. Even if, at the time, you were an unsuspecting baby. Even if, at the time, you merely wanted to get your baby baptized. Once you give God an opening, the door will never again be closed.

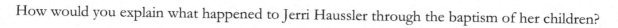

Questions for reflection:

How would you explain what happened to Jerri Haussler through the baptism of her children?

Have you ever found yourself doing unexpected things or responding to God's call in ways you wouldn't have considered a few years before? Explain.

Prayer: *Renew my faith, Lord. Call me back to the waters of renewal and new life. Amen.*

Day 5: Disciples

> *Matthew 4:18-22* *As he walked by the Sea of Galilee, he saw two brothers, Simon, who is called Peter, and Andrew his brother, casting a net into the sea-- for they were fishermen.* [19] *And he said to them, "Follow me, and I will make you fish for people."* [20] *Immediately they left their nets and followed him.* [21] *As he went from there, he saw two other brothers, James son of Zebedee and his brother John, in the boat with their father Zebedee, mending their nets, and he called them.* [22] *Immediately they left the boat and their father, and followed him.*

Jesus invested himself in 12 "disciples" (symbolic, perhaps, of the 12 tribes of Israel). Although Jesus taught large crowds of people, he worked intimately with the 12 disciples. What is a disciple? Here are a few definitions to consider:

Disciples learn to love God with their whole lives and love their neighbors as themselves.

Disciples learn to follow Jesus, learn to live the way of Jesus, learn to love and serve Jesus, and learn to let Jesus live through them (living by the Spirit).

A disciple is an "apprentice of Jesus who has been welcomed into Christian community through baptism: a lifelong learner of everything that Jesus taught; and one whose basic response to Jesus himself is obedience."[5]

"A disciple is one who responds in faith and obedience to the gracious call of Jesus Christ. Being a disciple is a lifelong process of dying to self while allowing Jesus Christ to come alive in us."[6]

Discipleship to Jesus Christ is "the intentional, communal, lifelong journey of being conformed to Jesus Christ through the power of the Holy Spirit to accomplish God's purpose in the world."[7]

Discipling is "a relationship where we intentionally walk alongside a growing disciple or disciples in order to encourage, correct and challenge them in love to grow toward maturity in Christ."[8]

Questions for reflection:

Is the word "disciple" too "churchy" or are you comfortable using the word to describe your own life?

Which definition of "disciple" catches your attention or resonates with you? Why?

Day 6: Vocation

> **2 Thessalonians 1:11-12** *To this end we always pray for you, asking that our God will make you worthy of his call and will fulfill by his power every good resolve and work of faith, [12] so that the name of our Lord Jesus may be glorified in you, and you in him, according to the grace of our God and the Lord Jesus Christ.*

For most of my life, when someone would ask me, what is your vocation or what is your occupation, I would give the same answer: pastor (assuming that my vocation and occupation were the same thing). I came upon a new understanding in a course taught by Dave Daubert. My current thinking is that every Christian shares the same vocation: we are disciples of Jesus Christ.

For Christians, our vocation is our daily ministry, drawn from our baptism. We live out our vocation in whatever roles we play (roles like pastor, or mother, or accountant, or student). "Pastor" is one of my roles; it is my occupation, not my vocation. My vocation is being a "disciple" of Jesus, and all Christians share this same vocation, to be about God's mission in the world through whatever roles and circles God places us. Our vocation involves "loving our spouse, caring for our children, talking to our next-door neighbor, doing our best in our daily work, being attentive to our co-workers, and making choices countless times each day to act with justice, kindness, and humility toward others."[9]

To: Jesus Ben Joseph

From: Management Consultants Incorporated

Dear Sir,

Thank you for submitting the resumes of the twelve men you have picked for positions in your new organization. All of them have now taken our battery of tests, and have completed the personal interviews with our psychologist and vocational aptitude consultant. It is the staff opinion that most of your nominees are lacking in background, education, and vocational aptitude for the type of enterprise you are undertaking. To begin, they do not have the team concept.

Simon Peter is emotionally unstable and given to fits of temper. Andrew has absolutely no qualities of leadership. The two brothers, James and John, place personal interest above company loyalty. Thomas demonstrates a questioning attitude that would tend to undermine morale. We feel that it is our duty to tell you that Matthew has been blacklisted by the Greater Jerusalem Better Business Bureau. James, the son of Alphaeus, and Thaddeaus definitely have radical leanings, and they both register a high score on the manic depressive scale.

We would recommend that you continue your search for persons of experience in managerial ability and proven capability. One of the candidates, however, shows great potential.

He is a man of ability and resourcefulness, meets people well, has a keen business mind and has contacts in high places. He is highly motivated, ambitious and responsible. We recommend Judas Iscariot as your controller and right-hand man.

Sincerely yours,
Management Consultants Incorporated[10]

Chances are, if we had to be interviewed and take a battery of tests, to be accepted by Jesus into the vocation of disciples, we also would not come highly recommended. For any number of reasons: stuck in sin, carrying heavy baggage, trying to put the broken pieces of life back together, or having difficulty denying and surrendering self. For any number of reasons, we may feel that we don't have much to offer when it comes to being light and salt and love and grace in the world around us. But the surprising thing is, if we're willing to be used by God, we will be used for God's purpose.

Questions for reflection:

How do you understand the "call" of God in your life, as the apostle Paul describes it in 2 Thessalonians 1:11 (above)?

In what roles do you live out your vocation? How does your vocation as a disciple impact these roles?

Close your devotions this week, returning to pray and meditate on the words of the *Prayer of Thanksgiving for Baptism*.

Taking It Further: Small Group and Chapter Summary Questions

(The questions at the end of each chapter have two purposes. If you are using this resource individually, these questions will help to summarize the week's study. If you are using this resource as a small group, these questions are a good starting point for group discussion. See the Preface: Small Group Guidelines for guidance about using these questions. If the small group has not yet developed a covenant, this first meeting would be a good time to do so.)

What kind of impact does your baptism have on your daily life?

Is the term "baptismal covenant" a new term for you or are you accustomed to talking about it?

Did you at some point in your life, consciously or unconsciously, enter into a baptismal covenant with God? Explain.

Do you think faith in God begins in a person both with and without baptism? Why do churches require baptism to become a church member?

Many Christians believe that God acts in baptism. What does God do?

How is baptism "free" or a means of "grace," if a covenant (about our responses to God) is attached to it?

It seems that the baptismal covenant is an under-utilized description of what it means to be a disciple. How can we be more intentional in our teaching children, youth, and adults about the baptismal covenant?

Is the baptismal covenant (the five promises) a thorough description of the Christian life? If yes, what is good about it? If not, what is missing?

Were you "confirmed" in the faith? If so, what do you remember about the program or the day of your confirmation? Did it have some importance or little or no significant impact upon you?

Do you think of yourself as a "disciple" of Jesus? Is it central to your identity or self-understanding? Why or why not? If so, how did you come to think of yourself in that way?

What questions or issues do you want to discuss further with others?

What Bible reading took on a new meaning for you?

What do you want to remember from this chapter?

Recommended resources for further study:

Daubert and Vos, *Reclaiming the "V" Word: Renewing Life at Its Vocational Core*

Foss, *Power Surge*

Fryer, *Reclaiming the "C" Word: Daring to Be Church Again*

Fryer, *Reclaiming the "L" Word: Renewing the Church from Its Lutheran Core*

Ogden, *Transforming Discipleship*

Chapter Two: Living Among God's Faithful People

Do you intend to continue in the covenant God made with you in holy baptism:
to live among God's faithful people,
to hear the word of God and share in the Lord's supper,
to proclaim the good news of God in Christ through word and deed,
to serve all people, following the example of Jesus,
and to strive for justice and peace in all the earth?"

THIS WEEK, we'll focus on the first promise of the baptismal covenant to live among God's faithful people. It is a promise to participate in the Body of Christ. (Why might this one be the first promise? Perhaps because it takes a community to raise a disciple.)

Day 1: *Koinonia*

Acts 2:42 *They devoted themselves to the apostles' teaching and fellowship, to the breaking of bread and the prayers.*

What does it mean to "live among God's faithful people?" The picture that best describes what it means to live among God's faithful people is found in Acts 2:42. "They devoted themselves to the apostles' teaching and fellowship, to the breaking of bread and the prayers."

There is a Greek word in that sentence that deserves closer study. The word "*koinonia*" in the New Testament is the gift of the Holy Spirit to the church. It refers first to the relationship we have with God through the Spirit and then to the relationships we have with each other through the Spirit. (There is both a vertical and a horizontal dimension to *koinonia*.) It refers to the oneness or unity we have in Jesus Christ (the unity Jesus prayed for his followers, that they would be one just as he and the Father were one – John 17:22-23). This unity is a gift of the Spirit, and we encourage its development among us when we open ourselves to the gift of the community.

Koinonia is translated as having fellowship with, being in communion with, being in close relationship with, being in partnership with, or being closely connected with. We see *koinonia* played out in Acts 2 as a complete sharing of life (including even a sharing of income and possessions so that all have their basic needs met).

What does it mean to live among God's faithful people? Turn to the entire passage, Acts 2:42-47, for a beautiful portrait of *koinonia*. They are in the Word together, learning and practicing the life Jesus taught. They are coming together in fellowship and enjoying meals together. They are meeting together in homes. They are helping to support each other. They are worshiping and praying together. Lives are being transformed. They are sharing their resources for the benefit of others. The Spirit of Jesus is noticeable in this community. There is a magnetism that is drawing other people to God.

That is a beautiful picture of what it means to live among God's faithful people. When you experience living in that kind of faith community, be sure to give thanks to God, because it is a gift of the Spirit.

Questions for reflection:

What do you think the investment of one's time has to do with the development of *koinonia*?

What other kinds of "investment" are helpful in building community?

Prayer: *Thank you, Lord, for the gift of my community of faith. Thank you for friends to walk with, for support and care, for love and honesty, for partnership and purpose. Amen.*

Day 2: Small Groups and Spiritual Growth

> ***Colossians 3:16*** *Let the word of Christ dwell in you richly; teach and admonish one another in all wisdom; and with gratitude in your hearts sing psalms, hymns, and spiritual songs to God.*

In August of 2010, I gave the congregation a questionnaire about spiritual growth (for my doctor of ministry research). 146 people completed the questionnaire. One question asked people what event, ministry, or experience has had a special impact on their spiritual growth. Many things were mentioned: worship, women's retreats, mission trips, serving others, participating on a ministry team, attending a church conference, or participating in a synodical lay school of theology course (ACTS).

But the most frequent mention, the most instrumental experience in the spiritual growth of people who responded to that questionnaire was their participation in a small group (a discipleship group, Bible study group, book study group, or LIFEKEYS group).[11] Small groups are God's gifts to encourage us to grow up in Christ. After 29 years as a pastor, I now say that small groups are an essential part of the makeup of the Christian church. Small groups are not just an additional activity for those who like them and who have the time; for any church that wants to grow in faith, spirit and mission, small groups are an essential part of the church.

Discipleship groups are a particular kind of small group. Three to four people meet together weekly for prayer, discussion about the biblical readings and workbook questions, fellowship and care for each other, and walking with each other in faith (in a word, *koinonia*). For many, their discipleship group experiences were life-changing. They developed the practice of reading the Bible. They became comfortable with talking about God and their faith. They became comfortable with praying aloud for and with each other.

We want to encourage many more people to participate in discipleship groups and other small groups. The more we avail ourselves to the opportunities of small groups (whether oriented to study, ministry, support, or serving), the more we open ourselves to receiving the gift of *koinonia*. And the more *koinonia* develops among us, the more we will resemble that Acts 2 community: worshiping together, praying together, studying the Word together, eating together, gathering together in homes, walking in the faith with each other, caring for each other, doing life together. And the Spirit of Jesus within the community becomes a magnetic force that draws other people who are hungering for an authentic community, people who want to experience how Christian love really works.

Questions for reflection:

How is life in your congregation similar or different to the life of the early Christian community in Acts 2:42-47?

Have you ever participated in a small group similar to that described above? If so, how has your involvement in small groups encouraged your spiritual growth?

If you have not participated in a small group, what do you think is the primary reason?

Day 3: Sharing Life and Resources

Acts 2:44-46 All who believed were together and had all things in common; [45] they would sell their possessions and goods and distribute the proceeds to all, as any had need. [46] Day by day, as they spent much time together in the temple, they broke bread at home and ate their food with glad and generous hearts...

Acts 6:1-6 Now during those days, when the disciples were increasing in number, the Hellenists complained against the Hebrews because their widows were being neglected in the daily distribution of food. [2] And the twelve called together the whole community of the disciples and said, "It is not right that we should neglect the word of God in order to wait on tables. [3] Therefore, friends, select from among yourselves seven men of good standing, full of the Spirit and of wisdom, whom we may appoint to this task, [4] while we, for our part, will devote ourselves to prayer and to serving the word." [5] What they said pleased the whole community, and they chose Stephen, a man full of faith and the Holy Spirit, together with Philip, Prochorus, Nicanor, Timon, Parmenas, and Nicolaus, a proselyte of Antioch. [6] They had these men stand before the apostles, who prayed and laid their hands on them.

There are several kinds of "sharing" that occur in the life of the early Christian community. Acts 2:44-46 mentions the sharing of financial resources and possessions as well as a sharing of meals in homes. It was the practice of the early church to gather together and celebrate the Lord's Supper as part of a shared meal. In this breaking of the bread, the community of faith shared not only their lives but also their provisions. "The meal was at once a practice of thanksgiving for the redemption offered in the new covenant, in the body and blood of Jesus; simultaneously, the meal was an economic practice, a practice of 'communion' with fellow believers, sharing their means."[12]

That is what is happening in Acts 6:1-6, when seven men are appointed to wait on tables for the daily distribution of bread to the widows. Here is the church living out the way of Jesus, sharing its provisions, meeting the needs in its midst. Early Christians evidently understood that the command to love one's neighbor meant to hold one's possessions loosely (Acts 4:32, 34), seeing the suffering of another as one's own suffering, and the burden of another as one's own burden.

Questions for reflection:

Can you think of examples today in which the church continues to live out the way of Jesus by sharing finances and resources?

Can you think of examples today in which the church continues to live out the way of Jesus by sharing meals and food with others?

Prayer: *Lord of all, turn our praises into hands that clothe the naked, arms that comfort the afflicted, tables that host the stranger, and shoulders that support the weary so that your name may be praised by all your people. Amen.*

Day 4: The Body of Christ

Romans 12:4-8 *For as in one body we have many members, and not all the members have the same function,* *⁵ so we, who are many, are one body in Christ, and individually we are members one of another.* *⁶ We have gifts that differ according to the grace given to us: prophecy, in proportion to faith;* *⁷ ministry, in ministering; the teacher, in teaching;* *⁸the exhorter, in exhortation; the giver, in generosity; the leader, in diligence; the compassionate, in cheerfulness.*

In 1 Corinthians 12, the Apostle Paul describes the Christian Church as the Body of Christ, using the imagery of the human body with its many parts. In that letter and in Romans 12, Paul presents the church as an interdependent organism. A body needs all its parts working together to function effectively. So in the community of faith, each member is in an interdependent relationship with all the other members. There are a diversity of people with a diversity of gifts, all of which are needed for the ministry and building up of the church. Each member relies on the gifts of others. Each member is involved in a giving and receiving relationship with the rest of the body. When one suffers, all suffer together; when one rejoices, all rejoice together.

There are over 50 references in the New Testament about how we are to relate to "one another" as the Body of Christ. If you would like to study these in more detail, this list is a good place to begin.

Love One Another: John 13:34-35; Romans 12:10; Galatians 5:13; Ephesians 4:2; Hebrews 10:24; Hebrews 13:1; 1 Peter 1:22; 1 Peter 3:8; 1 Peter 4:8; 1 John 3:11; 1 John 3:23; 1 John 4:7; 1 John 4:11; 1 John 4:12; 2 John 1:5.

Bearing with One Another; Forgive One Another: 1 Corinthians 12:25; Galatians 5:13; Ephesians 4:2; Ephesians 4:32; Colossians 3:13.

Be of One Mind with One Another: Romans 12:16; 1 Corinthians 1:10; 1 Thessalonians 5:13; 1 Peter 3:8.

Encourage One Another: 1 Thessalonians 4:18; 1 Thessalonians 5:11; Hebrews 3:13; Hebrews 10:24-25.

Come Together With One Another: Hebrews 10:25a; Romans 15:14; Ephesians 5:19; Colossians 3:16.

More "One Another" Commands: carry each other's burdens (Galatians 6:2); offer hospitality to one another (1 Peter 4:9); seek after what is good for one another (1 Thessalonians 5:15); clothe yourselves with humility toward one another (1 Peter 5:5); confess your sins to each other and pray for each other (James 5:16).

Questions for reflection:

How have you been blessed by the gifts of others in your church?

What gift(s) has God given you to contribute to the ministry of your faith community?

Prayer: *The gift of Christian community is a very precious gift! I give thanks to you, Lord, for my church, for my small group, and for the people who have blessed my life. Amen.*

Day 5: A Learning Community

Ephesians 4:11-16   The gifts he gave were that some would be apostles, some prophets, some evangelists, some pastors and teachers, [12] to equip the saints for the work of ministry, for building up the body of Christ, [13] until all of us come to the unity of the faith and of the knowledge of the Son of God, to maturity, to the measure of the full stature of Christ. [14] We must no longer be children, tossed to and fro and blown about by every wind of doctrine, by people's trickery, by their craftiness in deceitful scheming. [15] But speaking the truth in love, we must grow up in every way into him who is the head, into Christ, [16]from whom the whole body, joined and knit together by every ligament with which it is equipped, as each part is working properly, promotes the body's growth in building itself up in love.

In Ephesians 4:11-16, the author describes the gifting of church leaders (apostles, prophets, evangelists, pastors and teachers) by the Holy Spirit, for the purpose of equipping the people of God for their work of ministry and the building up of the Body of Christ.

Using the human body imagery, the author emphasizes the need for disciples to grow and mature, into the unity of the Spirit, into the knowledge of the Son of God, and into the fullness of Jesus Christ.

This passage and the larger context of Ephesians 4 present some characteristics of the maturing body of Christ: it maintains the unity of the Spirit; it uses the gifts of the Spirit to build up (edify) the people in Christ and to equip them for their ministry; it discerns truth from falsehood and speaks the truth in love; and it lives together in trusted relationships that reflect the love and forgiveness of Christ. These characteristics of the Christian community create the suitable environment for discipling of the body.

Disciples never cease growing in faith, but are forever responding to the God who calls them. The life of faith is not something one masters, but like baptism, it is a dynamic experience into which disciples continue to grow. It is an ongoing apprenticeship to Jesus, learning to live in his kingdom. God blesses us with a community of faith in which we learn together: "spiritual friends pray for and with each other, encourage each other, share insights into Scripture, and help one another reflect on the ways God is present and active in their lives."[13]

Questions for reflection:

Who are your spiritual friends? Who have served as spiritual mentors for you?

What experience have you had where you either gave or received "speaking the truth in love?" (Ephesians 4:15)

Prayer: *O Lord, whose patience is beyond comprehension, we thank you for the gift of the community of faith that we may walk together in our walk with you. We pray that you may never tire of helping us grow in faithfulness. Though we fail more than we succeed, raise us up each day to follow after you again. Amen.*

Day 6: A Community of Disciples

Luke 24:25-32   Then he said to them, "Oh, how foolish you are, and how slow of heart to believe all that the prophets have declared! [26] *Was it not necessary that the Messiah should suffer these things and then enter into his glory?"* [27] *Then beginning with Moses and all the prophets, he interpreted to them the things about himself in all the scriptures.* [28] *As they came near the village to which they were going, he walked ahead as if he were going on.* [29] *But they urged him strongly, saying, "Stay with us, because it is almost evening and the day is now nearly over." So he went in to stay with them.* [30] *When he was at the table with them, he took bread, blessed and broke it, and gave it to them.* [31] *Then their eyes were opened, and they recognized him; and he vanished from their sight.* [32] *They said to each other, "Were not our hearts burning within us while he was talking to us on the road, while he was opening the scriptures to us?"*

There are three actors in the process of making disciples: the Holy Spirit, the individual, and the community of faith. The Spirit, of course, is the primary actor; however, the Spirit chooses to work through the Body of Christ in forming the followers of Jesus. Disciples are best formed and nurtured within the community of faith.

In the story of the two disciples walking to Emmaus (Luke 24:13-35), consider how important is their experience of community. Although in sorrow, they are walking together. Their hearts burn within them as the "Stranger" interprets the Word of God for them. They recognize Jesus Christ as they break bread together at the table. Finally they run together to share the good news with the rest of the community in Jerusalem. I don't see how it is possible to live as a Christian apart from a community of faith.

We worshiped recently at a church in Iowa. We arrived at the church as another worship service was letting out. We entered the front doors of the church as others were leaving worship and heading for their cars. Although I looked into the faces of those leaving (ready to greet them), no one acknowledged me. No one looked at me. No one said "hello." As I sat down to prepare for worship, I wondered, how could Christians fail to acknowledge the other members of the body? And in what ways do we, do I, fail to acknowledge and respect the people of my own community of faith? In what ways do I overlook the presence and gifts of God in other people in our community?

Questions for reflection:

How important is it for members of a congregation to acknowledge and greet one another? Why?

Do you tend to recognize the presence of Jesus more in other people of your faith community or when you are alone?

Prayer: *God the Father, the Son, and the Holy Spirit, we pray for your church. Fill it with all truth and peace. Where it is corrupt, purify it; where it is in error, direct it; where in anything it is amiss, reform it; where it is right, strengthen it; where it is in need, provide for it; where it is divided, reunite it, as only you are able. Amen.*[14]

Taking It Further: Small Group and Chapter Summary Questions

What is your most memorable experience of close, authentic community?

Now that you have thought more about it, what does this promise mean to you:

I promise to live among God's faithful people?

How is this promise, "*I promise to live among God's faithful people*," both a gift and a promise?

How essential are small groups for a church that wants to grow disciples?

How does the foundation of community (the first promise) assist growth in living out the other promises of the baptismal covenant?

What are creative ways a faith community can share its resources so that all can have their basic needs met?

What significance should hospitality have for a community of faith?

What questions or issues do you want to discuss further with others?

What Bible reading took on a new meaning for you?

What do you want to remember from this chapter?

Recommended resources for further study:

Bilezikian, *Community 101*

Bonhoeffer, *Life Together*

Foss, *Power Surge*

Jones, *Traveling Together: A Guide for Disciple-Forming Congregations*

McDonald, *The Disciple Making Church: From Dry Bones to Spiritual Vitality*

Snyder, *Radical Renewal: The Problem of Wineskins Today*

Stanley, Willits, *Creating Community: Five Keys to Building a Small Group Culture*

Chapter Three: Hearing the Word of God

Do you intend to continue in the covenant God made with you in holy baptism:
  to live among God's faithful people,
  to hear the word of God and share in the Lord's supper,
  to proclaim the good news of God in Christ through word and deed,
  to serve all people, following the example of Jesus,
  and to strive for justice and peace in all the earth?"

GOD GIVES THE GIFT of God's Word so that we may know God, hear God, and follow in the way of Jesus. This week we'll focus on the first part of the second promise of the baptismal covenant, to hear the word of God.

Studying God's word is fundamental to the process of discerning, understanding, articulating, and applying the meaning of God's word in the life of a disciple. Studying God's word in community offers the opportunity to hear God speaking through others.

Day 1: Hearing the Word

> *John 6:68-69 Simon Peter answered him, "Lord, to whom can we go? You have the words of eternal life. [69] We have come to believe and know that you are the Holy One of God."*

Christian worship has a biblical foundation. The good news is proclaimed in scripture reading, preaching, and song. The first reading is usually taken from the Old Testament. A psalm may be read or sung in response to that reading. The second reading, usually from a New Testament letter, relates the witness of the early church. The Gospel (which means good news) is often introduced with the words of Peter to Jesus: "Lord, to whom shall we go? You have the words of eternal life." The Gospel then leads directly to the sermon.

Martin Luther considered preaching to be "the first of two peaks or high points in the worship service." Because the Holy Spirit works through the biblical readings and sermon to bring the Living Word to address us in our time and place, we should be prepared to hear God speak to the community and to us personally. Through the Word we are formed and empowered to "carry out the mission of God in our daily lives."[15]

Pastors and preachers are often amazed at the remarkable way the Holy Spirit can take the words of their sermons and use them to address particular issues in the lives of the worshipers, issues of which the preachers often have no particular knowledge. It's the same remarkable way the Spirit uses a reading in the Bible to speak God's Living Word to us today. Quite remarkable!

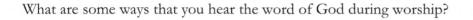

Questions for reflection:

What are some ways that you hear the word of God during worship?

What is one way you have heard the Living Word speak to you through the Bible?

Prayer: *Blessed Lord God, you have caused the holy scriptures to be written for the nourishment of your people. Grant that we may hear them, read, mark, learn, and inwardly digest them, that, comforted by your promises, we may embrace and forever hold fast to the hope of eternal life, which you have given us in Jesus Christ, our Savior and Lord. Amen.*[16]

Day 2: The Transforming Word of God

Romans 12:1-2 I appeal to you therefore, brothers and sisters, by the mercies of God, to present your bodies as a living sacrifice, holy and acceptable to God, which is your spiritual worship. ²Do not be conformed to this world, but be transformed by the renewing of your minds, so that you may discern what is the will of God-- what is good and acceptable and perfect.

Because the Bible was written over hundreds of years by many different authors and addressed to many different communities and cultures, the Bible needs to be interpreted. We do our best to understand the original message by the original author to the original audience before we seek to apply it to life today.

There will always be times when we read the Bible and interpret it differently.

There will be issues over which we disagree. As people of God we are invited to participate in an unending conversation with the Holy Spirit, the Bible, the tradition, and each other. We come to the scriptures in humility and prayer; rather than submitting the scriptures to our purposes, we seek to submit ourselves to the purposes of God in scripture.

We read the Bible, not so much for information, or knowledge, but for transformation. We read the Bible to be transformed, or in the words of the apostle Paul, to have Christ formed in us. The Scriptures are all about change. The Scriptures not only tell us about God changing people; the Scriptures themselves are used by God's Spirit to change us. The remarkable thing about the Bible is that God can use it to address us with his living Word, and we meet Jesus Christ, crucified and risen, and we are transformed. Through the Bible, God speaks to the core of our being, and we are changed.

Reflection (Ruth Poole)

It takes courage to take on the study of the Bible. Not because the reading is hard, but because it can change our lives.

Spending time in the Word takes desire, time, openness, commitment, determination and curiosity. A willingness to look beyond the obvious is almost a requirement. Satisfaction comes when a new perspective, a new insight, a new layer of understanding into God and God's plan for us is discovered. That then leads to our transformation.

Questions for reflection:

What are some potential reasons to study the Bible?

Why do you think hearing God's word read and proclaimed is considered an important part of the baptismal covenant?

Prayer: *When I come to read or hear your Word, Lord, may I come "under it," with humility and anticipation. Lead me, Lord, to desire in my heart to hear you speak. Give me courage, Lord, to be open to your work of transformation in my life. Amen.*

Day 3: The Desire

> *Psalm 119:33-35* *"Teach me, O LORD, the way of your statutes, and I will observe it to the end. Give me understanding, that I may keep your law and observe it with my whole heart. Lead me in the path of your commandments, for I delight in it."*

Psalm 119 describes an intimate relationship with God's Word. When you read through the psalm, you hear an assortment of verbs, which describe a special relationship between the author of the psalm and the Word of God. He walks in the word; he keeps it; he fixes his eyes upon it; he observes it; he treasures it; he delights in it; he meditates on it; he reveres it; he remembers it; he lives it; he declares it; he clings to it; his soul is consumed with longing for God's Word. What a beautiful relationship he enjoys with God's Word.

The Word of God guards his soul; it teaches him; it revives him; it leads him to understanding; it strengthens him; it blesses him; it keeps him from straying; it counsels him; it is a lamp unto his feet and a light unto his path. The Torah, the Word of God, is his guide for living for God; it is the way, the path. It leads to life.

What are we to do with the Bible? According to the author of Psalm 119, we are to be in a continuing conversation with it. We are to live with it. It is to be our mentor for living.

Reflection (Ruth Poole)

The desire to be in relationship with God is really the first requirement for daily Bible study. The Bible is simply the vehicle through which you can see, learn from and about God, and come to know God.

Making and keeping a daily appointment with God to spend time with Him strengthens your relationship with God. Just as spending time with your spouse, children or dog makes that relationship richer and stronger, spending daily time with God does the same or perhaps more. The time of day is less critical than the discipline of meeting God faithfully each day. There are those who strongly believe that their days are managed better when they have had their quality time with God in the early morning.

Be still (Psalm 46:10). Set aside the other thoughts of the day. Ask God to help you out here. A quiet place and a quiet mind create a welcoming environment for the presence of God. The stillness and the quiet allow God to speak through the study of scripture and through prayer.

Questions for reflection:

What does it mean to delight in the word (law) of the Lord? (Psalm 1:2)

Describe the relationship between the psalmist and the word of God. (Psalm 119: 9-16)

Do you currently spend time in God's Word? Daily? Weekly? If so, how has this practice impacted your life?

Prayer: *Lord, I call to you to hear me, but really I need to hear and know You. Quiet my mind, open my heart. Show me the way. In Christ, Amen.*

Day 4: Reading the Bible and the Bible Reading Us

> **Hebrews 4:12** *Indeed, the word of God is living and active, sharper than any two-edged sword, piercing until it divides soul from spirit, joints from marrow; it is able to judge the thoughts and intentions of the heart.*

As we read the Bible, we immerse ourselves in its story. We try to understand it in its context (seeking the intent of the author). We interpret the part in terms of the whole. We read it together, in conversation with the people of God, past and present. We read it in the context of prayer, allowing the Spirit to teach us.[17] We read the Bible, but that is not the only thing happening in the encounter.

The Bible also reads us. What do I mean? I'm referring to how when we are in the process of reading the Bible, we may think we are interpreting the Bible, but the Bible is interpreting us. Let's look at an example of how this happens in scripture itself. In 2 Samuel 11, we have the story of King David, walking upon the palace roof courtyard and seeing a lovely woman bathing some distance away. As king, he has come to think that he should have anything he desires. David makes the woman his own and has her husband killed by sending him to the frontlines of the battle.

In 2 Samuel 12, the prophet Nathan comes to David with a story. There were these two men, one of them a big-time rancher with large flocks and herds of livestock, and the other a poor man who owned just one little lamb. And this poor man had grown to love his little lamb and treated it as a member of the family rather than as a food source. (He would let it lap milk out of his own cereal bowl and sleep at the foot of his bed.) One day the rancher had a friend arrive unexpectedly for a visit, and instead of taking one of his own livestock, he "got somebody to go over and commandeer the poor man's lamb which he and his friend consumed" along with loaded baked potatoes and broccoli with hollandaise sauce.[18]

When David hears this, he explodes in anger. "As surely as God lives, the man who did this ought to die. At the least, he must repay for the lamb four times over for this crime!" And Nathan responds: "You are the man!" And here's what the God of Israel has to say to you. I made you king over Israel. I gave you your master's house and his daughter, and many other wives. I gave you both Israel and Judah. And if that hadn't been enough, I'd have gladly given you much more. Why have you despised the word of the Lord, doing this great evil? (And now because you have killed Uriah and taken his wife as your wife, because you have treated God with such contempt, killing will continually plague your family.)

David enters into Nathan's story, and when David pronounces condemnation on the rich farmer, little does he know that he is pronouncing his own condemnation. Nathan lets him have it: You are the man. (He is judged and found guilty.)

One of the ways the Bible reads us is to invite us into its own world so that we are drawn into its story and we see ourselves for who we are, we see the truth; we see ourselves in a new light. That's how the Bible reads us.

Questions for reflection:

In what Bible story or verse have you seen yourself?

What example can you remember from your own life where the Bible read you, that is, where you felt your own life held up in a mirror?

Day 5: How Does Jesus Approach Scripture?

Matthew 23:23-24 *Woe to you, scribes and Pharisees, hypocrites! For you tithe mint, dill, and cummin, and have neglected the weightier matters of the law: justice and mercy and faith. It is these you ought to have practiced without neglecting the others. 24 You blind guides! You strain out a gnat but swallow a camel!*

Matthew 5:17-20 *"Do not think that I have come to abolish the law or the prophets; I have come not to abolish but to fulfill. ¹⁸ For truly I tell you, until heaven and earth pass away, not one letter, not one stroke of a letter, will pass from the law until all is accomplished. ¹⁹ Therefore, whoever breaks one of the least of these commandments, and teaches others to do the same, will be called least in the kingdom of heaven; but whoever does them and teaches them will be called great in the kingdom of heaven. ²⁰ For I tell you, unless your righteousness exceeds that of the scribes and Pharisees, you will never enter the kingdom of heaven.*

Jesus seems to suggest that certain portions of scripture are weightier than others.

In Matthew 23:23, Jesus tells the Pharisees that they keep all their little regulations but neglect the weightier matters of God's word: justice, mercy and faith. (Which sounds very similar to Micah 6:8 – do justice, love mercy, and walk humbly with your God.) Jesus also accuses the Pharisees of ignoring the commands of God while over-valuing human traditions (Mark 7:8).

Jesus takes the whole of scripture and summarizes it in two commandments. That we love God above all else, with our highest commitment (all our heart and soul and mind and strength), and that we love our neighbors as ourselves (Matthew 22:34-40). Jesus teaches that the whole of God's instruction is concerned about a right relationship with God and with others. Jesus makes this the lens through which he reads all of scripture.

According to that principle, Jesus presses to the heart of the matter: "You have heard 'do not murder,' but I say to you do not be angry with your brother; do not insult or call him a fool. You have heard 'do not commit adultery,' but I say to you do not look with lust on another person.'" (Matthew 5 paraphrase) Jesus digs deeper into the intention of God rather than remaining satisfied with the observance of the external commandment. Everything comes back to the twofold love commandment: love God in everything you do and love your neighbor as well. Rather than observing the letter of the law, Jesus fulfills the spirit of God's intent.

Questions for reflection:

What examples have you seen where some scriptural verses are given more weight than you think they should receive?

What does Jesus' approach to scripture teach you?

Day 6: The Scriptures Point to Christ

2 Timothy 3:15-17 *"...and how from childhood you have known the sacred writings that are able to instruct you for salvation through faith in Christ Jesus. All scripture is inspired by God and is useful for teaching, for reproof, for correction, and for training in righteousness, so that everyone who belongs to God may be proficient, equipped for every good work."*

What is the purpose of scripture? The author of this New Testament letter writes that it is useful for teaching, correction, training, and equipping us for living. As we live with the Bible, it equips us for living for God in all we do.

Although verses 16-17 often receive most of the attention in this passage, Verse 15 of 2 Timothy 3 gets at what is the real purpose of the Bible: "how from childhood you have known the sacred writings that are able to instruct you for salvation through faith in Christ Jesus." (And what is most interesting here is that the "sacred writings" refer to the Old Testament.) Simply put, the Scriptures lead us to faith in Jesus Christ.

The gospels also point to this primary purpose of Scripture:

John 20:30-31 *"Now Jesus did many other signs in the presence of his disciples, which are not written in this book. But these are written so that you may come to believe that Jesus is the Messiah, the Son of God, and that through believing you may have life in his name."*

The Gospel is written to bring us to faith in Jesus the Lord and Savior and to life in his name.

Luke 24:44-48 *"Then Jesus said to them, 'These are my words that I spoke to you while I was still with you--that everything written about me in the law of Moses, the prophets, and the psalms must be fulfilled.'" Then he opened their minds to understand the scriptures, and he said to them, 'Thus it is written, that the Messiah is to suffer and to rise from the dead on the third day, and that repentance and forgiveness of sins is to be proclaimed in his name to all nations, beginning from Jerusalem. You are witnesses of these things.'"*

Jesus teaches his disciples that the law and prophets and writings of the Hebrew Scriptures all point to the Messiah, to the cross, to the proclamation of the good news of Jesus the Messiah, through whom God reconciles the world to himself. The Scriptures point us to Christ (to awaken faith in Christ). The Bible reveals Jesus Christ to us. "Eventually, everything in the Bible brings us to Jesus Christ. Everything in the Bible points us toward Christ and helps us to know Christ and to love Christ and to have a relationship with Christ, who is risen from the dead."[19]

Martin Luther liked to say that the Bible is like the manger that held the Christ child. Luther writes that reading the Bible is nothing else than Christ coming to us, or we being brought to him. As with everything else in the faith, the Bible is a means to a greater end. The creeds and confessions, the sacraments, Baptism and Holy Communion, the liturgy and praise songs, discipleship groups, "all of those things are important because they help us to have a relationship with Jesus Christ."[20]

The Bible is also a means to an end. "We do not disparage the Bible by saying that it always plays second fiddle to Jesus Christ. Rather, we value the Bible precisely because it brings us to Christ and keeps us grounded in Christ."[21]   This, especially for Lutheran Christians, is the primary purpose of the Bible. It presents Christ to us.

Questions for reflection:

Do you think the Bible is of human origin, divine origin, or both? Explain.

What might it mean to interpret scripture through the lens of Jesus Christ? (See John 5:39)

What leads you to think that God is speaking to you through the Bible, rather than your own ideas?

Taking It Further: Small Group and Chapter Summary Questions

What is your favorite verse, story, or book of the Bible? Why?

What do you treasure most about the Bible?

How is the statement, *I promise to hear the Word of God*, both a gift and a promise?

Discuss your reactions to these words by Soren Kierkegaard:

> "The Bible is very easy to understand. But we Christians are a bunch of scheming swindlers. We pretend to be unable to understand it because the minute we understand, we are obliged to act accordingly. Take any words in the New Testament and forget everything except pledging yourself to act accordingly. My God, you will say, if I do that my whole life will be ruined. How would I ever get on in the world? Herein lies the real place of Christian scholarship is the Church's prodigious invention to defend itself against the Bible, to ensure that we can continue to be good Christians without the Bible coming too close." [22]

What obstacles do you face when it comes to understanding the message of the Bible?

What is the most important purpose of Bible study?

What questions or issues do you want to discuss further with others?

What Bible reading took on a new meaning for you this week?

What do you want to remember from this chapter?

One of the benefits of using a devotional study guide like this one is that it encourages us to spend time in the Word regularly. What step might you take to meet God in his Word more regularly?

Describe a time you have felt the Holy Spirit spoke a message directly to you.

Recommended resources for further study:

Fee and Stuart, *How to Read the Bible for All Its Worth.*

Fee and Stuart, *How to Read the Bible Book by Book.*

Jacobson, Olson, Powell, *Opening the Book of Faith: Lutheran Insights for Bible Study.*

Karl Kuhn, *Having Words with God: The Bible as Conversation*

N.T. Wright, *The Last Word: Scripture and the Authority of God*

Chapter Four: Sharing in the Lord's Supper

Do you intend to continue in the covenant God made with you in holy baptism:
to live among God's faithful people,
to hear the word of God and share in the Lord's supper,
to proclaim the good news of God in Christ through word and deed,
to serve all people, following the example of Jesus,
and to strive for justice and peace in all the earth?"

ALONG WITH THE GIFT of a faith community, and the gift of God's Word, God also gives us the gift of grace in the Lord's Supper. This week we reflect on the gift of worship, and in particular the Lord's Supper. "Worship is the linchpin of a discipleship church. It is in the gathering of God's people around Word and Sacrament that the community of faith affirms its calling, receives the gifts of grace, is nourished and strengthened, and sent back into the world to love as God loves."[23]

Day 1: Worship

> **Mark 12:29-30** *Jesus answered, "The first is, 'Hear, O Israel: the Lord our God, the Lord is one;* [30] *you shall love the Lord your God with all your heart, and with all your soul, and with all your mind, and with all your strength.'"*

When Jesus identifies the greatest commandment as devoting our whole selves to God above all else, he sets worship at the center of human life. In *"Soul Feast: An Invitation to the Christian Spiritual Life"* Marjorie Thompson writes, "Worship, a full-hearted love of God, is meant to permeate our lives. Private or public, it is always first and foremost a matter of the heart…True worship from the heart means responding to God's glory and love with our entire being."[24]

Worship is the appropriate response to who God is.[25] When we become aware of who God really is, the appropriate response is to turn and yield our whole being, heart, soul and mind and strength. That is worship. Worship invites us to take our attention away from ourselves and redirect it toward God.[26] In other words, the focus of worship is God. "The core of worship is when one's heart and soul, and all that is within, adores and connects with the Spirit of God."[27]

Worship can be informal or formal, public or private. Worship can take place in a church sanctuary and in a car, in nature and almost anywhere. When we talk about hearing the word of God and sharing in the Lord's Supper, we are referring to worship within the gathered Body of Christ. Sometimes public worship is defined as the things we do for God. (The word *liturgy* comes from the Greek word *leitourgia*, which simply means the service or the work of the people.) In this sense, worship is the "work" of all the faithful who gather to praise, honor, and glorify God.

We also define corporate worship by the gifts God gives us: the word and the sacraments: baptism and communion. In worship we receive these gifts of God's grace, through which Christ is present with us. In these means of grace, the Spirit renews, forgives, and speaks to us, and we experience the presence of the triune God.

Questions for reflection:

Do you think of worship more as something God does for you or you do for God?

Where does your worship of God most often happen?

Prayer: *Everywhere I am, Lord, everywhere I look, I see signs of your handiwork, signs of your presence, and signs of your love. May I see you even more clearly, and love you even more dearly, today and tomorrow. Amen.*

Day 2: Words of Institution

> *1 Corinthians 11:23-26* *For I received from the Lord what I also handed on to you, that the Lord Jesus on the night when he was betrayed took a loaf of bread,* [24] *and when he had given thanks, he broke it and said, "This is my body that is for you. Do this in remembrance of me."* [25] *In the same way he took the cup also, after supper, saying, "This cup is the new covenant in my blood. Do this, as often as you drink it, in remembrance of me."* [26] *For as often as you eat this bread and drink the cup, you proclaim the Lord's death until he comes.*

In many Christian worship services, before the Lord's Supper is shared, the pastor or elder leads the congregation in the Eucharistic Prayer, or Communion Prayer, a prayer of thanksgiving to God. We thank God for creation, for God's faithfulness to the people of ancient Israel, and for God's saving work in Jesus Christ.[28] In this prayer we welcome the host of the meal, the Lord Jesus Christ, and we hear again his words about his body broken and his blood poured out for the world. We call these words, the **Words of Institution**, the words of Jesus as he instituted the Lord's Supper at the last supper with his disciples.

> *In the night in which he was betrayed,*
> *our Lord Jesus took bread, and gave thanks;*
> *broke it, and gave it to his disciples, saying:*
> *Take and eat; this is my body, given for you.*
>
> *Do this for the remembrance of me.*
>
> *Again, after supper, he took the cup, gave thanks,*
> *and gave it for all to drink, saying:*
> *This cup is the new covenant in my blood,*
> *shed for you and for all people for the forgiveness of sin.*
>
> *Do this for the remembrance of me*[29].

In these Words of Institution we hear the story of the last supper and the meaning of the Lord's Supper as we continue to celebrate it. Jesus identifies the bread and wine as his body and blood that are broken and shed for the world. In this new covenant of forgiveness, we receive the blessings and benefits of his death and resurrection.

The biblical readings and sermon proclaim the word of God in an audible way. The Lord's Supper proclaims the word of God in a different way, by taste. We receive the gospel in bread and wine. Martin Luther called the celebration of the Lord's Supper the second "high point" of worship. "In the Word read and proclaimed, God speaks to us." The **Lord's Supper** is the visible word in which God feeds us with the presence of Jesus Christ.[30]

The meal draws us into a communion with God and a communion with each other (and with the world). The Holy Spirit gathers and forms us into the Body of Christ around God's gifts of grace: the Word of God and the Lord's Supper. In the Body of Christ we are connected to the larger community of faith, and we are reminded who we are and whose we are.

We become the body of Christ as we receive the bread and wine. The transforming work of the Holy Spirit in us empowers us to become broken bread and poured-out wine for the life of the world.

The phrase we use to describe the mystery of the meal is that we receive the "real presence" of Jesus Christ, in, with, and under the elements of bread and wine. Christ comes to us in very tangible, material things, to transform us. This is a wonderful mystery.

Questions for reflection:

How important is it for you to receive communion in a church worship service?

What word of promise do you hear spoken to you in the Words of Institution?

What do you think it means to proclaim the Lord's death (1 Corinthians 11:26)?

Prayer: Lord, "reveal yourself to us in the breaking of the bread. Raise us up as the body of Christ for the world. Breathe new life into us. Send us forth, burning with justice, peace, and love."[31] Amen.

Day 3: Shed for You and for All People

> *1 Peter 1:18-19 You know that you were ransomed from the futile ways inherited from your ancestors, not with perishable things like silver or gold, [19] but with the precious blood of Christ, like that of a lamb without defect or blemish.*

"One day a little girl asked her father why he always carried a little piece of flat metal in his pocket. Her father smiled warmly, sat down with his daughter and began to explain, 'Honey, during World War II my company was under heavy attack. The fighting was fierce! I was in a fox hole with four of my closest buddies. All of a sudden a hand grenade came tumbling in. All of us would have been killed had it not been for Tom. He threw himself onto that grenade and absorbed the explosion with his body. Tom gave his life for his friends. From that day to this I have carried his dog tags in my pocket. Whenever I touch them, I remember his loving sacrifice for me, how he died so I might live."[32]

In a similar way, when we receive the bread and taste the wine, we taste the gospel of Jesus Christ: his sacrificial death for the world. We taste the depth of God's love for humankind. We taste the bitter agony of the cross for us. We taste the refreshing gifts of grace and forgiveness. We taste the newness of life, that because he died, we live.

Question for reflection:

What does it mean to you that the blood of Christ was shed for you?

Prayer: *"Holy God, holy and mighty, holy and immortal: you we praise and glorify, you we worship and adore….With this bread and cup we remember your Son, the first-born of your new creation. We remember his life lived for others, and his death and resurrection, which renews the face of the earth. We await his coming, when, with the world made perfect through your wisdom, all our sins and sorrows will be no more. Amen. Come, Lord Jesus."[33]*

Day 4: For the Forgiveness of Sin

> *Matthew 26:26-29   While they were eating, Jesus took a loaf of bread, and after blessing it he broke it, gave it to the disciples, and said, "Take, eat; this is my body."* [27] *Then he took a cup, and after giving thanks he gave it to them, saying, "Drink from it, all of you;* [28] *for this is my blood of the covenant, which is poured out for many for the forgiveness of sins.* [29] *I tell you, I will never again drink of this fruit of the vine until that day when I drink it new with you in my Father's kingdom."*

Martin Luther draws our attention to two phrases in the proclamation of the Lord's Supper: "for you" and "forgiveness of sins." In his Large Catechism, Luther writes: "we go to the sacrament because there we receive a great treasure, through and in which we obtain the forgiveness of sins. Why? Because the words are there and they impart it to us! …Therefore, it is appropriately called food of the soul, for it nourishes and strengthens the new creature…the Lord's Supper is given as a daily food and sustenance so that our faith may be refreshed and strengthened and that it may not succumb in the struggle but become stronger and stronger. For the new life should be one that continually develops and progresses."[34]

Communion is a meal for us, for all; food for faith; food for our soul. In this meal, our forgiveness is proclaimed, and we taste the Word of Life.

Reflection (Irene Cernik)

In Lutheran worship the sacrament of communion is central. By the celebration of the Lord's Supper we participate in the meal Jesus himself instituted, the meal "that is poured out for many for the forgiveness of sins." The sacrifice of Christ is the grounds for forgiveness. God's forgiveness is limitless and complete; He remembers sins no more.

As sharers in the Lord's life and death we are empowered to "go and do likewise." Practicing forgiveness begins with self examination, especially before worship, a time of honest assessment of who we are in the sight of God. Revealing our need for true confession, not self-condemnation, we trust in the Holy Spirit to guide us. Then, we are freed to accept God's grace.

How often have we entered worship with a feeling of superiority, with a fresh retaliation under our belts, with bitterness carried in the soul, firmly clutching a long held hurt? Unforgiveness will ultimately poison us, not the one from whom we withhold forgiveness. Petitioning God's forgiveness will reveal the need to go further. Not all situations require our personal contact with the unforgiven person.

A turning point came to me after the death of a loved one. Hurt and bitterness served as my constant companions with regard to this person. Labeling those feelings as "unforgiveness" came to me through the Holy Spirit. Only after reading God's word and hearing His desires and willingly following His lead could my selfish motives heal. Throughout my life the Lord's Prayer played a central role, and now it does so with meaning and conviction on my part. Forgive us our sins *as we forgive others.*

Questions for reflection:

Is the word of God's forgiveness something that ought to occur in every worship service? Explain.

What does it mean to you that the Communion words "for you" are spoken directly to you from Jesus Christ the host of the meal?

Do you find yourself challenged when you pray, "forgive us our sins as we forgive those who sin against us?" Is there a past hurt that you still hang on to? Offer it to God in prayer.

Prayer: *We give you thanks, O Lord, that you refresh us through the healing power of the gift of grace. May this grace so work in us that we become graceful persons toward our neighbors, our friends, and even our enemies. Amen.*

Day 5: Do This for the Remembrance of Me

> *1 Corinthians 10:16-17 The cup of blessing that we bless, is it not a sharing in the blood of Christ? The bread that we break, is it not a sharing in the body of Christ? [17] Because there is one bread, we who are many are one body, for we all partake of the one bread.*

"Like the disciples, in the breaking of the bread, we recognize the presence of the risen Jesus Christ"[35] (Luke 24:30-31). Through this meal we are brought into communion with Jesus Christ, and with each other. We are forgiven and given new life. God nourishes us and forms us into the Body of Christ for God's mission in the world. We are fed with Christ and filled with love to go out to love and serve our neighbors.

The final part of the worship service, following communion, is the "sending." The pastor "blesses us in the name of God, granting us God's favor and peace. With the blessing of God we go out to live as Christ's body in the world, proclaiming the good news that the kingdom of heaven has come near, living in service to others, caring for all in need, and continuing our participation in God's mission," until we are gathered once again around the gifts of God: the Word of God and the Lord's Supper.[36]

In the communion celebration, the past, present, and future come together:

Past: We recall the Lord sharing the Passover meal with his disciples and instituting the Lord's Supper.

Present: We experience the real presence of Jesus Christ in the present meal.

Future: And we also look into the future as we anticipate the return of Jesus Christ and the full consummation of the kingdom of God. Each gathering of the Body of Christ around the Lord's table anticipates the heavenly banquet, when we will join with all of God's people in the final renewal of all creation.

Past...present...future.

Christ has died...Christ is risen...Christ will come again.

Questions for reflection:

What is one way you can live out the "remembrance" of Christ?

How have you experienced communion as a glimpse of the heavenly banquet?

How does Holy Communion strengthen your faith?

Prayer: *"O God, we give you thanks that you have set before us this feast, the body and blood of your Son. By your Spirit strengthen us to serve all in need and to give ourselves away as bread for the hungry, through Jesus Christ our Lord. Amen."*[37]

Day 6: Living Eucharistically

> *1 Thessalonians 5:16-18* *Rejoice always,* [17] *pray without ceasing,* [18] *give thanks in all circumstances; for this is the will of God in Christ Jesus for you.*

The word "Eucharist" is from a Greek word that means thanksgiving. The Lord's Supper is also called the Eucharist, Holy Communion, and the Sacrament of the Altar. "Eucharist" reminds us that it is a meal of thanksgiving. The "Altar" language reminds us of the sacrifice of Christ for us. The "Lord's Supper" reminds us that the risen Lord Jesus is the host, and we anticipate being reunited at the heavenly banquet. Finally, "Communion" recalls that we experience the real presence of Jesus Christ, and that we also are formed into the Body of Christ as we come together at the meal.

To live eucharistically is to live with an attitude of thanksgiving. Just as Jesus took the bread, broke it, gave thanks, and gave it to all, so we receive and acknowledge each gift with gratitude. For the Jews in Jesus' day, everything in God's creation was understood to be a gift from God to be enjoyed, and for which one would thank God.

To live eucharistically:

- is to see everything in life as an occasion for thanking God;
- is to acknowledge that what you have, you have receive from another;
- is to give credit where credit is due;
- is to live life in praise and thanks to God;
- is to say "thank you" to God with your life.

Questions for reflection:

For what do you give thanks when you receive the gifts of bread and wine?

How do you say "thank you" to God with your life?

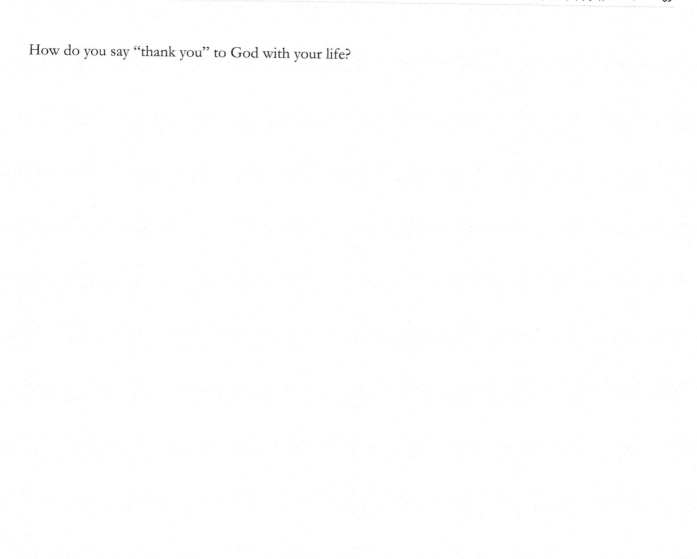

Prayer: *Almighty God, you provide the true bread from heaven, your Son, Jesus Christ our Lord. Grant that we who have received the sacrament of his body and blood may abide in him and he in us, that we may be filled with the power of his endless life, now and forever. Amen.*[38]

Taking It Further: Small Group and Chapter Summary Questions

How is the statement, *I promise to share in the Lord's Supper*, both a gift and a promise?

When during the worship service do you most feel the presence of God?

How are the word (spoken) and the meal (eaten) similar and different?

What makes worship, worship?

Which phrase in the Words of Institution carries a special meaning for you? Why?

What questions or issues do you want to discuss further with others?

What Bible reading took on a new meaning for you this week?

What do you want to remember from this chapter?

Recommended resources for further study:

Evangelical Lutheran Worship: "Narrative Holy Communion"

Thompson, *Soul Feast: An Invitation to the Christian Spiritual Life*

Chapter Five: Proclaiming the Good News through Words and Deeds

Do you intend to continue in the covenant God made with you in holy baptism:
to live among God's faithful people,
to hear the word of God and share in the Lord's supper,
to proclaim the good news of God in Christ through word and deed,
to serve all people, following the example of Jesus,
and to strive for justice and peace in all the earth?"

JESUS PROCLAIMED THE GOOD NEWS of the kingdom of God in words and deeds. He announced God's intention to restore shalom and reconcile the world to himself, and his works of healing and deeds of love demonstrated that this restoration was possible here and now. When Jesus hands over his mission to his disciples after the resurrection (Matthew 28:19; Luke 24:47-48; John 20:21-23; Acts 1:8), he commissions them to continue to proclaim the good news of God's kingdom in words and deeds.

Day 1: Living Stones of Testimony (Deb Meyers)

Joshua 4:19-24 The people came up out of the Jordan on the tenth day of the first month, and they camped in Gilgal on the east border of Jericho. ²⁰ Those twelve stones, which they had taken out of the Jordan, Joshua set up in Gilgal, ²¹ saying to the Israelites, "When your children ask their parents in time to come, 'What do these stones mean?' ²²then you shall let your children know, 'Israel crossed over the Jordan here on dry ground.' ²³ For the LORD your God dried up the waters of the Jordan for you until you crossed over, as the LORD your God did to the Red Sea, which he dried up for us until we crossed over, ²⁴ so that all the peoples of the earth may know that the hand of the LORD is mighty, and so that you may fear the LORD your God forever."

1 Peter 2:4-10 Come to him, a living stone, though rejected by mortals yet chosen and precious in God's sight, and like living stones, let yourselves be built into a spiritual house, to be a holy priesthood, to offer spiritual sacrifices acceptable to God through Jesus Christ. For it stands in scripture: "See, I am laying in Zion a stone, a cornerstone chosen and precious; and whoever believes in him will not be put to shame." To you then who believe, he is precious; but for those who do not believe, "The stone that the builders rejected has become the very head of the corner," and "A stone that makes them stumble, and a rock that makes them fall." They stumble because they disobey the word, as they were destined to do. But you are a chosen race, a royal priesthood, a holy nation, God's own people, in order that you may proclaim the mighty acts of him who called you out of darkness into his marvelous light. Once you were not a people, but now you are God's people; once you had not received mercy, but now you have received mercy.

In Joshua, we read that the Israelites set up stones of remembrance when crossing into the Promised Land so that in generations to come, when children would ask what the stones meant, the elders could give testimony to who God is and what He had done for them.

In 1 Peter we read that Jesus is the living stone, a living reminder or testimony to us of the extravagant love of God for you and me and all people. And it says we too are like living stones (v.5). We are a chosen people belonging to God so that we may declare the praises of him who called us out of darkness and into his wonderful light. (v.9).

Our lives are to be living testimonies that God is real, that he is alive and still at work in the world; that he still loves, forgives, heals and transforms broken lives. And yes, he is still in the business of calling even the most unlikely and unexpected people to be his witnesses.

My mom had a profound impact on my faith. Her faith saw her through some very difficult times. In the last month of her life, when my brothers and sisters and I were caring for her while she battled cancer, we saw her faith shining through in such powerful and profound ways. She found the strength in God to count her blessings instead of her sorrows every single day. She taught us how to LIVE with cancer, how to die with grace, and that God was her sustainer in every-single circumstance of life. The hospice workers saw it, her friends and co-workers saw it, her kids and grandkids saw it. God used her as a witness to his sustaining power and extravagant love, right up to her last breath. She was a living stone of testimony, and her living and dying in faith has impacted the faith of the next three generations of her family.

Question for reflection:

How are you a living testimony of the extravagant love of God, to your kids, grandkids, friends, and extended family? (Never question for a moment when, where, or how God might use you.)

Prayer: *God I praise you for your unfailing love, your sustaining power and grace. Work in me so that I might be a living stone of testimony to all I encounter. In Christ's name I pray. Amen.*

Day 2: It's Time (Deb Meyers)

In our Baptismal Covenant we are called to "proclaim the good news in word and deed." As disciples of Jesus, we are called to "*be* the voice to speak the good news." These very words are painted on our church sanctuary wall at Peace, as a constant reminder.[39]

Do you feel a sudden urge to close this book or skip ahead to next week's devotions at the very mention of this topic? Maybe you want to put your hands over your ears and say "lalalalalalala" real loud so you don't hear the call to proclaim the good news. It's scary. We probably would prefer to leave this job to the paid church professionals. We may feel ill-equipped for the job or might have had some really negative experiences in the past that make us resistant to this idea altogether. Have you said to yourself, "I don't feel called to do this" or "this is not my area of giftedness? You are not alone if you're thinking, "I just don't want to! I don't have the words. I can't."

"But it's time." That's what Kelley Fryer suggests in her book, *Reclaiming the "E" Word.*. "It's time for us to share the really good news about God's loving mission to save, heal, forgive, reconcile, and set free the whole creation and every single person in it. It's time for us to get out the word about Jesus, who sought after and welcomed those who had been cast aside, who shared his table with everyone, no questions asked and no exceptions made, whose radical, reckless love has torn down every wall that separates us from God and from each other. It's time for us to dare to deliver a message this world is dying to hear."[40]

> *Isaiah 43:10* says "You are my **witnesses**," declares the LORD, "and **my servant** whom I have chosen, **so that you may know and believe me** and understand that I am he. Before me no god was formed, nor will there be one after me."

We have been given the incredible privilege and gift to know God and believe God. We all have areas of brokenness in our lives, yet Jesus reminds us that we are loved with unfailing love; that we are chosen, blessed, accepted and forgiven. That he's the God who has the power to transform broken lives and restore us to wholeness.

We live in a broken world, where news of man's inhumanity to man dominates news headlines; where we are daily bombarded with stories of war, starvation, murder and disaster; stories of greed, corruption and the misuse of power. The world is in desperate need of the news we have to share: that it doesn't have to be this way. Jesus teaches us a better way to live. He works within us through the power of the Holy Spirit to transform not only our lives but our world.

It's time. Time to understand that the gift of unconditional love and grace we receive is a call to discipleship, to follow the way of Jesus. It's time, to step out in faith and trust that God can and will walk with us, guide us to the people and circumstances where he wants us to act and will supply the necessary words of love, acceptance, forgiveness and encouragement when they are needed. "Imagine how the lives of our friends, family, coworkers, and schoolmates, would change if we dared to let God shower them with love and hope and joy through the story that we have to tell. Imagine how the world would change if we began sharing the really good news with our neighbors without embarrassment and without hesitation."[41]

Questions for reflection:

What images come to mind when you think about an "evangelist?"

What thoughts come to mind when you think of yourself as a "witness?"

Prayer: *Lord, please take my fear, insecurity, and resistance to being your witness. Forgive me for all the missed opportunities of the past. When it comes to talking about you, change my "I don't want to and I can't" to "I want to and You can." Open my eyes to the people you place in my path today, who may need to hear a bit of Your good news. Supply the words you want me to speak. Guide my actions so that others might see Jesus working through me and be drawn to You. Strengthen my trust and my faith in You, to help me be a good witness to the good news You have for all people. Amen.*

Day 3: Word and Deed

> **Matthew 9:9-13** *As Jesus was walking along, he saw a man called Matthew sitting at the tax booth; and he said to him, "Follow me." And he got up and followed him. [10] And as he sat at dinner in the house, many tax collectors and sinners came and were sitting with him and his disciples. [11] When the Pharisees saw this, they said to his disciples, "Why does your teacher eat with tax collectors and sinners?" [12] But when he heard this, he said, "Those who are well have no need of a physician, but those who are sick. [13] Go and learn what this means, 'I desire mercy, not sacrifice.' For I have come to call not the righteous but sinners."*

Proclaiming the good news about Jesus Christ in **our words** means being willing to share our faith story. It means being open to the possibility of a spiritual conversation. It means taking your faith with you wherever you go and being open to the possibilities to speak a word of hope or comfort to another person. (Often the best "witnessing" or sharing one's faith comes out of caring listening and attending to the needs of others.)

When you talk to another person about Jesus, you are helping that person take the next step toward Jesus. That's what the tax collector Matthew did. He invited his friends to dinner to meet Jesus for themselves.

Proclaiming the good news about Jesus in **our deeds** will be the subject matter of the next three chapters (serving others and striving for peace and justice in the world). "Our neighbors and friends outside the Christian church will be persuaded, not by clarity of doctrine or the preaching of the pastor, but through living discipleship. When they see adults, young people and children striving to live their faith and open to discussing what they believe and why," the good news of Jesus is being proclaimed.[42]

Roy Hattersly, an outspoken atheist, lamented that the people showing up to help in the relief efforts after Hurricane Katrina seemed to be only Christian groups. He didn't see teams from rationalists' societies, free thinkers' clubs or atheists' associations ("the sort of people who scoff at religion's intellectual absurdity"). Christians are the people most likely to make the sacrifice involved in helping others.[43]

Both words and actions are important in witnessing. Together they provide an integrity that cannot help but be noticed. Not only our words, but our lives become places where God speaks.

Questions for reflection:

In Matthew 5:13-16, Jesus calls his disciples "salt" and "light." When Jesus says we are to be the salt of the earth and the light of the world, what do you think he means?

Is it easier for you to use words or deeds when pointing to Jesus? Why?

Day 4: My Story about God

1 Peter 3:15-16   Always be ready to make your defense to anyone who demands from you an accounting for the hope that is in you; yet do it with gentleness and reverence.

Suppose you were given an assignment to write a few paragraphs about God. Where would you start? You might start with some Bible stories and verses. You might also include some words about God that you know from your own experience. Guess what...that *is* your assignment. Below are some questions to trigger some responses.

People – Whom has God used in your life to draw you to himself? How did God use them in your life?

Events – Can you point to significant events in your life which were pivotal events for your spiritual formation?

Baptism?

Confirmation?

Youth Group?

Retreat?

Birth of a Child?

Worship Moment?

Small Group?

Other Events?

What have been the biggest blessings in your life? How did/didn't you see God in these?

What have been the biggest challenges or difficult times in your life? How did/didn't you see God in these?

When and where did you most sense God's presence or guidance in your life?

When and where did you most sense God's power or work in your life?

When did you feel God was carrying you, the time(s) when you were most needing to rely on God?

Prayer: *As I look back on my life, Lord, I see your hand guiding me, upholding me, and lifting me up. Thank you for all the ways and times your presence has sustained me. Amen.*

Day 5: More about My Story about God

> *2 Corinthians 4:5-7 For we do not proclaim ourselves; we proclaim Jesus Christ as Lord and ourselves as your slaves for Jesus' sake. [6] For it is the God who said, "Let light shine out of darkness," who has shone in our hearts to give the light of the knowledge of the glory of God in the face of Jesus Christ. [7] But we have this treasure in clay jars, so that it may be made clear that this extraordinary power belongs to God and does not come from us.*

Choose one of the statements below (or revise one or write one of your own) and use it as the theme to write down a portion of your story about God.

- My life has been a steady life-long growing in God's grace.
- I can think of a few key events that helped to turn me toward God.
- In retrospect, I can see God's hand, presence, and guidance in and over my life through this time.
- God was able to bring about good and growth where I would never have expected it.
- These were times when I came to understand more about Paul's words in 2 Corinthians 12:7-10, that God's grace is sufficient for me…that when I am weak, God is strong.
- I have experienced a deepening of my love for Jesus.
- When I look at my life the last few years, I see a growth in generosity and compassion that can only have come from God.
- I'm coming to understand my life more and more as coming from God and going toward God.
- Though I struggle and wonder if I'm making any progress, I keep returning to the truth that God loves me, and that is enough.
- How has Jesus changed my life?

Use this space to write a portion of your story about God.

Day 6: Actions Speak Louder than Words (Deb Meyers)

> ***James 1:22-25*** *But be doers of the word, and not merely hearers who deceive themselves. [23] For if any are hearers of the word and not doers, they are like those who look at themselves in a mirror; [24] for they look at themselves and, on going away, immediately forget what they were like. [25] But those who look into the perfect law, the law of liberty, and persevere, being not hearers who forget but doers who act-- they will be blessed in their doing.*

In our baptismal covenant we are to proclaim the Good News in word AND deed. We've all heard the old adage: "Actions speak louder than words." If there is incongruity between the two, people will believe what they see rather than what they hear. This is especially true in living a life of faith. Jesus warned people and pointed out hypocrisy, and that warning still applies to us today.

Long before I knew what it meant to follow Jesus, my grandparents, Ed and Anna Bruns, served as living role models for what that actually looks like in real life. I remember accompanying them to the community baseball field one Saturday morning when I was young. We carried mops, brooms, a bucket and bleach. Much to my surprise (and distaste), we ended up cleaning the park toilet facilities. I can remember asking a number of questions. Did they get paid to do it? No. Were they filling in for someone else who was paid to do it? No. Had anyone asked them to do it? No. Why were we doing it? Because it needed to be done and the health and safety of the children in town was important to them. To my knowledge, no one in the community ever knew who cleaned the bathrooms. But when families gathered for little league games, the bathrooms were always clean.

Grandma was always sewing clothing for the children of seminary students. She knew how hard it must be to support a family while going to school. Grandpa worked to better the small farming community, by leading the campaign to build a medical clinic.

When oil was discovered on a farm my grandparents owned in Kansas, I overheard their discussion on how the money from it would be divided. God would get a third, grandpa would get a third and grandma would get a third. I was present when the first check arrived. Their eyes got really big when they opened the envelope. I never discovered the check amount, but there is no doubt in my mind that God ended up getting much more than a third. They both had a passion for helping people in need.

They both loved Jesus and they told stories of how God had faithfully seen them through the ups and downs of life - the lean years of the great depression, the death of their only son at the age of 3, Grandpa's survival from surgery to remove a kidney when my mom was still a little girl. They saw God's faithfulness in all circumstances.

In James, we are told that we shouldn't just listen to the word of God, but do what it says. Our lives, our actions, our choices, our priorities, our words and our stories all serve as sign posts to God.

Questions for reflection:

Who are the people in your life whose actions and words reflect God in their lives?

Are there areas of your life that you would like to change in order to be a better faith role model for others? (Take time today to reflect on that question, and as you think of areas in which you'd like to grow, ask God to help you.)

Taking It Further: Small Group and Chapter Summary Questions

What is your personal experience with "evangelism?" Do you shy away from the word? Do you shy away from the activity?

Do you most often feel anxious, embarrassed, eager, overwhelmed, ill-equipped, or excited to share your faith and tell about Jesus? (Circle one and explain.)

How has God used your life or your story to influence others?

Have you ever considered that you might be the one to change someone's negative stereotypes of what it means to be a Christian?

What person in the circles of your life might you intentionally listen to, in hopes that a spiritual conversation might develop?

Does witnessing to Jesus have to mean that all other religions are condemned or wrong?

What questions or issues do you want to discuss further with others?

What Bible reading took on a new meaning for you this week?

What do you want to remember from this chapter?

Recommended resources for further study:

Bliese and Van Gelder, *The Evangelizing Church: A Lutheran Contribution*

Bowen, *Evangelism for "Normal" People: Good News for Those Looking for a Fresh Approach*

Fryer, *A Story Worth Sharing: Engaging Evangelism*

Fryer, *Reclaiming the "E" Word: Waking Up to Our Evangelical Identity*

Richardson, *Reimagining Evangelism: Inviting Friends on a Spiritual Journey*

Chapter Six: Serving All People

Do you intend to continue in the covenant God made with you in holy baptism:
to live among God's faithful people,
to hear the word of God and share in the Lord's supper,
to proclaim the good news of God in Christ through word and deed,
to serve all people, following the example of Jesus,
and to strive for justice and peace in all the earth?"

THIS WEEK WE'LL FOCUS on the fourth promise of the baptismal covenant, to serve all people following the example of Jesus. God's gifts of community, word and meal, equip us to participate in God's love for the world.

Jesus turned the values of the world upside down when he identified serving with greatness. "Success and greatness are defined by the world in terms of status, wealth and power. Jesus calls his followers to set aside their own interests and well being in favor of the interests and well being of others."[44]

Day 1: Do with Me What You Want (Lore Amlinger)

> *Mark 8:34-37 He called the crowd with his disciples, and said to them, "If any want to become my followers, let them deny themselves and take up their cross and follow me. [35] For those who want to save their life will lose it, and those who lose their life for my sake, and for the sake of the gospel, will save it. [36] For what will it profit them to gain the whole world and forfeit their life? [37] Indeed, what can they give in return for their life?*

Once we acknowledge that we are not masters of our own lives, we are on the way to discipleship. Since our society is largely based on a ME-mentality, and our own natural self is also seeking satisfaction and gratification, there are quite a few obstacles to overcome before we are on the path to servanthood. Pride and ambition stand in the way. What is a successful life in the eyes of the world: making a name for yourself, rising on the corporate ladder, power, wealth, influence, having the right connections? Of course there is nothing inherently wrong in wanting to acquire knowledge in a field and to excel in it. After all, God has given all of us talents to develop and use. But growth in a human sense should not be all. How easy it is to think I really have too much on my own plate, I really don't have time to devote to the needs of others. I am doing all I can and maybe one day when I am less busy I will be able to reach out. Way down deep I knew that this is what I should do if I consider myself to be a Christian.

Knowing how to act as a servant is one thing, but that is not enough. Love without action is hollow (just as action without love). And what a striking practical example we have in the story of the foot-washing (John 13). Not only are the roles of master and disciple reversed, the Lord either must have bent down or even kneeled in front of the disciples; the task itself is such menial labor.

Servanthood requires service without holding back and makes demands on our time and talents. Giving of oneself can include so many things, visiting shut-ins, bringing a meal to a sick neighbor, driving others to church and appointments, writing a note to a friend who needs cheering up; even a phone call can brighten someone's day. No special talents required, easy to do, but following Christ also can be hard and requiring sacrifice.

Questions for reflection:

How are servanthood and discipleship connected?

What is one thing you have learned from serving another person?

Prayer: *O Lord, I put myself completely into your hands. Do with me what you want! You have created me for yourself...I want to be what you want me for. I want to follow you and only am asking you for strength for this day.*[45]

Day 2: The Humility of Service

John 13:12-17   *After he had washed their feet, had put on his robe, and had returned to the table, he said to them, "Do you know what I have done to you? [13] You call me Teacher and Lord-- and you are right, for that is what I am. [14] So if I, your Lord and Teacher, have washed your feet, you also ought to wash one another's feet. [15] For I have set you an example, that you also should do as I have done to you. [16] Very truly, I tell you, servants are not greater than their master, nor are messengers greater than the one who sent them. [17] If you know these things, you are blessed if you do them.*

Through serving others, we learn humility. We learn to notice and care about the needs of others. Through serving, we learn to give up our own rights and privileges, maybe even our desire to be in control. "Gathered at the Passover feast, the disciples were keenly aware that someone needed to wash the others' feet. The problem was that the only people who washed feet were the least. So there they sat, feet caked with dirt. It was such a sore point that they were not even going to talk about it. No one wanted to be considered the least. Then Jesus took a towel and a basin and redefined greatness. Having lived out servanthood before them, he called them to the way of service: 'If I then, your Lord and Teacher, have washed your feet, you also ought to wash one another's feet. For I have given you an example, that you also should do as I have done to you' (John 13:14, 15)."[46]

In service, says Richard Foster, we "experience the many little deaths of going beyond ourselves."[47] Serving enables us to say No to the world's games of self-promotion, to the world's estimation of greatness. Service leads us to quietly and unpretentiously go about caring for the needs of others. "More than any other single way, (says Richard Foster) the grace of humility is worked into our lives through the discipline of service."[48]

When we are involved in service that is hidden, that does not call attention to the service rendered, we step away from the power of our pride and give up our right to be in charge. We learn to be available and vulnerable. Service reinforces the truth of the cross, that the call to follow Jesus is to deny ourselves and take up our cross; to follow his agenda rather than doing or getting what we want.

Questions for reflection:

What do you think about this distinction: volunteering is about our own convenience; servanthood is about "laying down our lives."[49]

How can serving another person be a "freeing" experience?

Prayer: *Dear Lord, you have called us to be your servants. Open our eyes to see the needs around us and our hearts to lend a helping hand. Amen.*

Day 3: Upside-Down Kingdom

Jesus had previously taught his disciples that what is considered great in the kingdom of God is very different from what is considered great in the world. The disciples had stumbled over this issue a few times, for example, when they argued over which of them was greatest. And again when James and John asked for special positions of prominence in Jesus' kingdom.

These arguments became teachable moments. Jesus gathered the disciples together and said to them:

> *"You know that among the Gentiles those whom they recognize as their rulers lord it over them, and their great ones are tyrants over them. But it is not so among you; but whoever wishes to become great among you must be your servant, and whoever wishes to be first among you must be slave of all. For the Son of Man came not to be served but to serve, and to give his life a ransom for many."* (Mk 10:42-45)

Jesus taught his disciples that greatness equals service and humility. In God's kingdom, the great person is the one who is servant of others. Jesus, the Lord, came to serve. Followers of Jesus will take on his example and his character; they will also be ones who serve, who give their lives for others.

Mother Teresa said: "We can do no great things, just small things with great love. It is not how much you do, but how much love you put into doing it."[50]

Question for reflection:

The messages of the world around us suggest that we deserve to be served. Jesus, to the contrary, teaches us to serve others. Describe a way that you struggle with this tension.

Prayer: *Teach us, Lord, to live in your kingdom. Teach us to see with your eyes and hear with your ears. Then may we serve others as you call us. Amen.*

Day 4: The Ministry of Helpfulness

> ***Philippians 2:1-5*** *If then there is any encouragement in Christ, any consolation from love, any sharing in the Spirit, any compassion and sympathy, ² make my joy complete: be of the same mind, having the same love, being in full accord and of one mind. ³ Do nothing from selfish ambition or conceit, but in humility regard others as better than yourselves. ⁴ Let each of you look not to your own interests, but to the interests of others. ⁵ Let the same mind be in you that was in Christ Jesus…*

Richard Foster draws a distinction between choosing to serve and choosing to be a servant. "When we choose to serve, we are still in charge. We decide whom we will serve and when we will serve. And if we are in charge, we will worry a great deal about anyone stepping on us, that is, taking charge over us. But when we choose to be a servant, we give up the right to be in charge. There is great freedom in this. If we voluntarily choose to be taken advantage of, then we cannot be manipulated. When we choose to be a servant, we surrender the right to decide who and when we will serve. We become available and vulnerable."[51]

In his book, *Life Together*, Dietrich Bonhoeffer writes about the ministry of helpfulness. "Nobody is too good for the lowest service. Those who worry about the loss of time entailed by such small, external acts of helpfulness are usually taking their own work too seriously. We must be ready to allow ourselves to be interrupted by God, who will thwart our plans and frustrate our ways time and again, even daily, by sending people across our path with their demands and requests. We can, then, pass them by, preoccupied with our more important daily tasks, just as the priest—perhaps reading the Bible—passed by the man who had fallen among robbers. When we do that, we pass by the visible sign of the cross raised in our lives to show us that God's way, and not our own, is what counts."[52]

Questions for reflection:

What is one helpful way to think less about yourself and more about others?

What's the difference between an interruption in your day and a "divine appointment" where God sends someone across your path? Have you experienced any "divine appointments?" Explain.

Prayer: Are you serious about following Jesus as your Lord? Do you want your life to more closely resemble the life of Jesus? Then consider beginning each day with this simple prayer: *"Lord Jesus, as it would please you bring me someone today whom I can serve."*[53]

Day 5: Getting Out of the House

> ***Romans 13:8-10*** *Owe no one anything, except to love one another; for the one who loves another has fulfilled the law.* [9] *The commandments, "You shall not commit adultery; You shall not murder; You shall not steal; You shall not covet"; and any other commandment, are summed up in this word, "Love your neighbor as yourself."* [10] *Love does no wrong to a neighbor; therefore, love is the fulfilling of the law.*

Standing on the door step of Bilbo Baggins's house, the wizard Gandalf tells Bilbo that he is looking for someone to share in an adventure that he is arranging, and it's difficult to find anyone. Bilbo responds: "I should think so — in these parts! We are plain quiet folk and have no use for adventures. Nasty disturbing uncomfortable things! Make you late for dinner! I can't think what anybody sees in them."[54]

Sixty years later, as his nephew Frodo Baggins and Sam set out on an adventure to take the magic ring out of the Shire, Frodo remembers what his uncle Bilbo Baggins once told him: "It's a dangerous business going out your door. You step onto the road and if you don't keep your feet, there's no knowing where you might be swept off to."

Jim Wallis is the founder and editor of Sojourners Journal, a Christian journal concerned with fighting social injustice. Wallis writes that we all realize something is wrong in our world. But in order to have an impact on our world or community, we first have to understand it. "To understand it usually requires a change in our thinking. And for that to happen, we have to experience more of the world than we can know inside the comfortable confines of our lives. We have to cross the barriers that divide people and, indeed, that separate whole worlds from one another."[55]

We have to overcome the "ingrained cultural conditioning that keeps people in their own world and prevents them from experiencing another one."[56] I think that's true. People who are passionate about and involved with social change can often point back to a time when they first went to a third world country, or even just across town to the inner city. "There, in a world very different from their own, they had conversion experiences that would shape the rest of their lives."[57] The first step in making a difference in your world or your community is to leave your house. To escape your comfort zone and experience a different reality. This getting out of the house applies not only to individuals, but also to churches.

Questions for reflection:

Can you remember a time in your life where "poor" or "lower income" took on a face? Explain.

Describe a time when you "left your house" (or comfort zone) and discovered something unexpected?

Day 6: When Poverty Has A Face

Romans 12:9-13 *Let love be genuine; hate what is evil, hold fast to what is good;* [10] *love one another with mutual affection; outdo one another in showing honor.* [11] *Do not lag in zeal, be ardent in spirit, serve the Lord.* [12] *Rejoice in hope, be patient in suffering, persevere in prayer.* [13] *Contribute to the needs of the saints; extend hospitality to strangers.*

Dale Recinella was an international lawyer who lived in Florida. He was accustomed to arranging financing on multi-million and even billion-dollar deals for corporations, banks and governments. One day something changed his life. He began to help out at the noon meal of the Good News Soup Kitchen in Tallahassee. Soon he was showing up every day in his 3 piece suit from 11AM until 1:30 PM. He was assigned door duty. His job was to ensure that the street people lining up to eat waited in an orderly fashion. Every day he stood at the door for an hour, chatting with the street people waiting to eat.

One evening Recinella happened to be standing at a street corner when he noticed a lonely figure limping by on the nearby corner. He tells the rest of the story this way: "I was about to turn back to my own concerns when I detected something familiar in that shadowy figure. The red scarf. The clear plastic bag with the white border. The unmatched shoes. (It was Helen, a woman that he had talked with at lunch earlier in the day.) My eyes froze on her as she limped by and turned up the street. No doubt she would crawl under a bush to spend the night. My mind had always dismissed the sight of a street person in seconds. But it could not expel the picture of Helen."[58]

"That night as I lay on my fifteen-hundred-dollar deluxe temperature-controlled waterbed, I couldn't sleep. A voice in my soul kept asking, 'Where's Helen sleeping tonight?' No street person had ever interfered with my sleep. But the shadowy figure with the red scarf and plastic bag had followed me home. I had made a fatal mistake. I had learned her name."[59]

"That's what happens when you get involved. You learn people's names, and that makes all the difference. Poverty is no longer just a social or economic problem when you have a personal friend who is poor."[60]

Now this attorney devotes his energies and skills to helping overcome poverty. Instead of multi-million dollar deals, he puts together multi-sector partnerships to help move families out of poverty.

"It is a beautiful thing when folks in poverty are no longer just a missions project but become genuine friends and family which whom we laugh, cry, dream, and struggle… Servanthood is a fine place to begin, but gradually we move toward mutual love, genuine relationships."[61]

Questions for reflection:

What reasons or excuses do you find most useful in refraining from "getting involved?"

The Jesuit Volunteer Corps, which sends young people into inner city and rural poverty areas for a year of service, has this motto: 'Ruined for life!' The idea behind it is that once you've seen real poverty and gotten your feet wet by doing something about it, you won't ever be the same again. You'll be ruined for life.[62] What do you think they mean by that statement?

Prayer: *God of compassion, whose Son became poor for our sake: Help us to see the face of Christ in those who are poor, and in serving them to serve you. Give us generous hearts so that those living in poverty may have adequate food, clothing, and shelter. By your Spirit move us to affirm the dignity of all people and to work for just laws that protect the most vulnerable in society, through Jesus Christ, our Savior and Lord. Amen.*[63]

Taking It Further: Small Group and Chapter Summary Questions

What thoughts come to mind when you hear this promise of the baptismal covenant: *"I promise to serve all people following the example of our Lord Jesus?"*

Whom do you admire for putting the needs of others above his or her own? Which of his or her characteristics would you like to have?

Describe an experience of serving others that was pivotal in your life. What did you learn from it?

What can bother you most about serving others?

Discuss your reactions to this statement by Dietrich Bonhoeffer: "One can joyfully and authentically proclaim the Word of God's love and mercy with one's mouth only where one's hands are not considered too good for deeds of love and mercy in everyday helpfulness."[64]

What do you think about Richard Foster's distinction between choosing to serve and choosing to be a servant?

Which of the Bible readings took on a new meaning for you this week?

What questions or issues do you want to discuss further with others?

What do you want to remember from this chapter?

Recommended resources for further study:

Bonhoeffer, *Life Together*

Claiborne, *The Irresistible Revolution: Living As an Ordinary Radical*

Foster, *Celebration of Discipline: The Path to Spiritual Growth*

Sorenson and DeGrote-Sorenson, *Let the Servant Church Arise*

Wallis, *Faith Works: How to Live Your Beliefs and Ignite Positive Social Change*

Chapter Seven: Striving for Justice in All the Earth

Do you intend to continue in the covenant God made with you in holy baptism:
  to live among God's faithful people,
  to hear the word of God and share in the Lord's supper,
  to proclaim the good news of God in Christ through word and deed,
  to serve all people, following the example of Jesus,
  and to strive for justice and peace in all the earth?"

Christians are called to pursue both mercy and justice. In the mission of mercy (often called social ministry), we give of our time, talents and resources to help those in need. In the mission of justice, we seek to address the root causes that cause people to be deprived of their basic needs.

One way of proclaiming the good news of God in Christ through our words and deeds is by speaking and acting for justice in our community and world. This week and next week we'll focus on the final promise of the baptismal covenant, **striving for justice and peace in all the earth.**

Day 1: God Has a Song

God has a song. It permeates the Scriptures. God begins singing this song to the patriarchs, Abraham, Isaac, Jacob, and Joseph: "I will be your God, and you will be my people. I will give you your own land. I will bless you so that through you the whole world will be blessed."

In Exodus chapter 3, we hear more of God's song, and we learn that the song is about God's compassion for his people. God sings the song to Moses: "I have observed the misery of my people who are in Egypt; I have heard their cry on account of their taskmasters. Indeed, I know their sufferings, and I have come down to deliver them from the Egyptians, and to bring them up out of that land to a good and broad land, a land flowing with milk and honey…" (Exodus 3:7-8)

The God of the Bible is a God of justice, a God who executes justice for those without power and means: the orphan, the widow, and the stranger.

> *"Happy are those whose help is the God of Jacob, whose hope is in the LORD their God, who made heaven and earth, the sea, and all that is in them; who keeps faith forever; who executes justice for the oppressed; who gives food to the hungry. The LORD sets the prisoners free; the LORD opens the eyes of the blind. The LORD lifts up those who are bowed down; the LORD loves the righteous. The LORD watches over the strangers; he upholds the orphan and the widow, but the way of the wicked he brings to ruin." (Psalm 146:5-9)*

Later in the Scriptures, God cues in the prophets to add harmony to the song.

Micah sings this verse: "He has told you, O mortal, what is good; and what does the LORD require of you but to do justice, and to love kindness, and to walk humbly with your God?" (Micah 6:8)

Amos sings along: "Take away from me the noise of your songs; I will not listen to the melody of your harps. But let justice roll down like waters, and righteousness like an ever-flowing stream." (Amos 5:23-24)

Isaiah sings about the coming servant of the Lord, whom God will send to bless the afflicted, the broken-hearted, the captives, the prisoners, and those who mourn. (Isaiah 61:1-3)

The song of Mary that we call the Magnificat adds another verse to God's song. Mary's song breaks forth when she visits her relative, Elizabeth, and receives confirmation from Elizabeth that what the angel has told her about the child Mary is carrying is true. She sings: "My soul magnifies the Lord, and my spirit rejoices in God my Savior, for he has looked with favor on the lowliness of his servant." What begins as a song of praise to God, describes God as a God who remembers the poor and lowly and delivers them from the proud and oppressive: "God has shown strength with his arm; he has scattered the proud in the thoughts of their hearts. He has brought down the powerful from their thrones, and lifted up the lowly; he had filled the hungry with good things, and sent the rich away empty." (Luke 1:46-55)

When Jesus begins his ministry in Luke's gospel, he begins it by singing God's song. Jesus picks up the tune from Isaiah 61. In his hometown synagogue, Jesus unrolls the scroll and reads from Isaiah: "The Spirit of the Lord is upon me, because he has anointed me to bring good news to the poor. He has sent me to proclaim release to the captives and recovery of sight to the blind, to let the oppressed go free, to proclaim the year of the Lord's favor." After sitting down Jesus says: "Today this scripture has been fulfilled in your hearing." (Luke 4:17-21)

Two chapters later, Jesus (in 4 beatitudes) proclaims God's blessing on the poor, the hungry, those who weep, and those who are hated, excluded and reviled on account of Jesus. (Luke 6:20-23)

Jesus comes into the world to bring about God's realm of *shalom*, where the hungry are fed, the sick are healed, sinners are forgiven, prisoners are released, the poor hear good news, the rich joyfully give away their possessions, enemies are loved, all people share the bounty of God's earth, humans live in unity with all of nature, and all creation worships the creator Lord.[65]

God's kingdom reaches out to everyone. No one is beyond the blessing of God. That is the song of God that Jesus sings.

Questions for reflection:

How would you distinguish between the mission of mercy and the mission of justice? How are they related?

Can you summarize the song of God (about justice for God's people) in a sentence or two?

Prayer: *Look with mercy, gracious God, upon people everywhere who live with injustice, terror, disease, and death as their constant companions. Rouse us from our complacency and help us to eliminate cruelty wherever it is found. Strengthen those who seek equality for all. Grant that everyone may enjoy a fair portion of the abundance of the earth; through your Son, Jesus Christ our Lord. Amen.*[66]

Day 2: Speaking Truth to Power

Nehemiah 5:1-13 Now there was a great outcry of the people and of their wives against their Jewish kin. ² For there were those who said, "With our sons and our daughters, we are many; we must get grain, so that we may eat and stay alive." ³ There were also those who said, "We are having to pledge our fields, our vineyards, and our houses in order to get grain during the famine." ⁴ And there were those who said, "We are having to borrow money on our fields and vineyards to pay the king's tax. ⁵ Now our flesh is the same as that of our kindred; our children are the same as their children; and yet we are forcing our sons and daughters to be slaves, and some of our daughters have been ravished; we are powerless, and our fields and vineyards now belong to others." ⁶ I was very angry when I heard their outcry and these complaints. ⁷ After thinking it over, I brought charges against the nobles and the officials; I said to them, "You are all taking interest from your own people." And I called a great assembly to deal with them, ⁸ and said to them, "As far as we were able, we have bought back our Jewish kindred who had been sold to other nations; but now you are selling your own kin, who must then be bought back by us!" They were silent, and could not find a word to say. ⁹ So I said, "The thing that you are doing is not good. Should you not walk in the fear of our God, to prevent the taunts of the nations our enemies? ¹⁰ Moreover I and my brothers and my servants are lending them money and grain. Let us stop this taking of interest. ¹¹ Restore to them, this very day, their fields, their vineyards, their olive orchards, and their houses, and the interest on money, grain, wine, and oil that you have been exacting from them." ¹² Then they said, "We will restore everything and demand nothing more from them. We will do as you say." And I called the priests, and made them take an oath to do as they had promised. ¹³ I also shook out the fold of my garment and said, "So may God shake out everyone from house and from property who does not perform this promise. Thus may they be shaken out and emptied." And all the assembly said, "Amen," and praised the LORD. And the people did as they had promised.

Although it promises blessing to the down-and-out, God's song is not always received gladly. Sometimes people are offended, especially those who have an investment in keeping things the way they are. When we're among those benefiting from the good life, we may see nothing wrong with the status quo — we are comfortable with the way the world is. However, "though the world may be tilted toward the rich and powerful," God is tilted toward the down-and-out.[67]

God's song is somewhat subversive; it seeks to upset the status quo. There are verses in God's song that say the first will be last and the last will be first. Those who humble themselves will be exalted, and those who exalt themselves will be humbled.

"When people begin moving beyond charity and toward justice and solidarity with the poor and oppressed, as Jesus did, they get in trouble. Once we are actually friends with folks in struggle, we start to ask why people are poor, which is never as popular as giving to charity. One of my friends has a shirt marked with the words of late Catholic bishop Dom Helder Camara: 'When I fed the hungry, they called me a saint. When I asked why people are hungry, they called me a communist.' Charity wins awards and applause, but joining the poor gets you killed."[68]

While serving as governor following his successful rebuilding project of the city walls and gates, Nehemiah challenged the most powerful people about the way they were using their wealth to take advantage of the workers in their community. The wealthy were lending money and charging excessive interest (usury). When the debtors would miss a payment, the lenders would take over their fields. Then left with no means of income, the debtors would sell their children into slavery.

At this large assembly, Nehemiah addresses the powerful people: "The thing that you are doing is not good.... Let us stop this taking of interest. Restore to them, this very day, their fields, their vineyards, their olive orchards, and their houses, and the interest on money, grain, wine, and oil that you have been exacting from them." (5:9-11)

It may be hard for us Americans to understand this, but Nehemiah is hearkening back to the ethic of the Torah in which the community is to care for one another, and see to it that all have what they need, as a higher value than seeking personal gain. That is hard for us to imagine. The surprising thing is that the wealthy, powerful people respond to Nehemiah. They say, "We will restore everything and demand nothing more from them. We will do as you say."

Each year through our partnership in IMPACT (the local partnership of over 30 congregations working for justice in Charlottesville) we hold a modern day Nehemiah Assembly (usually in March) to address an issue of injustice in our own community.

Questions for reflection:

Why is working for justice more threatening than working for mercy?

What might lead those in power to treat the poor with compassion?

We affluent North Americans think we're entitled to our lifestyle... why would we want to change the system? How might that kind of thinking be part of the problem?

Prayer: *Lead me, Lord, to recognize that I cannot live in a just society until all those around me also live in a just society. Amen.*

Day 3: The Kingdom of God is a Kingdom of Justice

Isaiah 61:1-3 *The spirit of the Lord GOD is upon me, because the LORD has anointed me; he has sent me to bring good news to the oppressed, to bind up the brokenhearted, to proclaim liberty to the captives, and release to the prisoners; ² to proclaim the year of the LORD's favor, and the day of vengeance of our God; to comfort all who mourn; ³ to provide for those who mourn in Zion-- to give them a garland instead of ashes, the oil of gladness instead of mourning, the mantle of praise instead of a faint spirit. They will be called oaks of righteousness, the planting of the LORD, to display his glory.*

The entire biblical message could be summarized as God's desire for *shalom* for all creation. From the original garden in Genesis to the new heaven and new earth in Revelation, God is creating or recreating a "kingdom" of wholeness, abundance, welfare, harmony, peace, and justice (interrelated realities that are also interdependent; one leads to the other; and one is needed for the others to exist.)

As God the Father is a God of justice, so is Jesus the Son. In the synoptic gospels, Jesus announces the arrival of the kingdom of God and invites people to enter into the kingdom. In his inaugural sermon in Luke 4, Jesus quotes the prophet Isaiah, announcing that the mission given to him by the Father would be about justice: "The Spirit of the Lord is upon me, because he has anointed me to bring good news to the poor. He has sent me to proclaim release to the captives and recovery of sight to the blind, to let the oppressed go free, to proclaim the year of the Lord's favor." (Luke 4:18-19)

In Jesus, God's kingdom comes among us to bring about *shalom*, goodness, forgiveness, liberation, reconciliation, and justice. The word "kingdom" can be misleading: it is neither a place, nor a political system. Jesus comes into the world to bring about God's reign of *shalom*, where "the hungry are fed, the sick are healed, sinners are forgiven, prisoners are released, the poor hear good news, the rich joyfully give away their possessions, enemies are loved, all people share the bounty of God's earth, humans live in unity with all nature, and all creation worships the creator Lord."[69]

In Jesus the restoration of God's creation has begun. The words of Jesus, his miracles and healings, and the cross and resurrection, demonstrate that God's reign has arrived. The church is invited to participate in that mission now even as it anticipates the final consummation sometime in the future. The book of Acts of the Apostles (especially 2:42-47 and 4:32-37) presents the early church community as a community of faith that embodies the call of its Lord to live as kingdom people, characterized by alternative values and communal concern and provision for all in need.

Questions for reflection:

Are you a hopeful person? If so, what causes you to be a hopeful person?

What signs do you see of God's kingdom of *shalom* expanding? Offer a prayer of thanks for these signs of God's work among us.

Day 4: Complicity

Leviticus 19:9-10 When you reap the harvest of your land, you shall not reap to the very edges of your field, or gather the gleanings of your harvest. 10 You shall not strip your vineyard bare, or gather the fallen grapes of your vineyard; you shall leave them for the poor and the alien: I am the LORD your God.

As we have mentioned, the Christian Church does a better job with mercy than with justice. "We have cared for the oppressed, but have often failed to confront the oppressor. Tolerance of injustice, and even unholy alliances with exploiters of the people, are among the great sins of Christian history that have often contributed to tyranny and war. When considering injustice it is well to begin with confession of our own sins and not just the sins of others."[70]

Archbishop Oscar Romero preached that the church needs to stand with the poor and oppressed, because that is where God is. "There is one rule by which to judge if God is with us or is far away – the rule that God's word is giving us today: everyone concerned for the hungry, the naked, the poor, for those who have vanished in police custody, for the tortured, for prisoners, for all flesh that suffers, has God close at hand. The guarantee of one's prayer is not in saying a lot of words. The guarantee of one's petition is very easy to know: How do I treat the poor? –because that is where God is. The degree to which you approach them, and the love with which you approach them, or the scorn with which you approach them—that is how you approach your God. What you do to them, you do to God. The way you look at them is the way you look at God."[71]

Questions for reflection:

What impact does your lifestyle have upon the rest of the world? (Offer to God in a prayer of confession what comes to mind.)

How can one begin to address the large seemingly overwhelming problems of injustice in the world?

Day 5: Making a DIFFERENCE – Making an IMPACT (Tom Czelusta)

2 Corinthians 8:1-6 We want you to know, brothers and sisters, about the grace of God that has been granted to the churches of Macedonia; ² for during a severe ordeal of affliction, their abundant joy and their extreme poverty have overflowed in a wealth of generosity on their part. ³ For, as I can testify, they voluntarily gave according to their means, and even beyond their means, ⁴ begging us earnestly for the privilege of sharing in this ministry to the saints– ⁵ and this, not merely as we expected; they gave themselves first to the Lord and, by the will of God, to us, ⁶ so that we might urge Titus that, as he had already made a beginning, so he should also complete this generous undertaking among you.

Something led the Macedonians to respond to the needs of the poor with a deep generosity, in spite of their own poverty. "Can overfed, comfortably clothed, and luxuriously housed persons understand poverty? Can we truly feel what it is like to be a nine-year-old boy playing outside a village school he cannot attend because his father is unable to afford the books? Can we comprehend what it means for poverty-stricken parents to watch with helpless grief as their baby daughter dies of a common childhood disease because they, like at least one-quarter of our global neighbors today, lack access to elementary health services? Can we grasp the awful truth that thirty-four thousand children die every day of hunger and preventable diseases?"[72]

What does it take to make a difference, to make an impact?

A spirit of initiative – seeing a need and acting to fill it,
A sense of responsibility – a willingness to be responsible for our own actions and inaction,
Personal authenticity – one whose words speak truly of who they are,
Generosity – giving of what we have to give,
And the ability to risk – to risk failure and ridicule, a willingness to stand alone if necessary…

Guided by …

A living faith – a faith that is reflected by the totality of our daily life,
Hope - from the knowledge that the Spirit will not take us where the grace of God cannot keep us,
Love – the giving of ourselves to reach in and touch the heart of another as Christ would,
Humility – the quality that teaches us that every person is special and unique in God's eyes, no matter how twisted or battered they have become.

God calls us to participate in God's mission of restoring God's *shalom* in God's world. We look forward with yearning, for the time when humanity will embrace the blessing which God intended from the very beginning. When Jesus will return to judge the world, bringing an end to injustice and restoring all things to God's original intent for *shalom*. When God will reclaim and restore this world and rule forever. "On that day we will beat swords into tools for cultivating the earth, the wolf will lie down with the lamb, there will be no more death and God will wipe away all our tears. Our relationship with God, others, ourselves, and creation will be whole. All will flourish as God intends. This is what we long for. This is what we hope for. And we are giving our lives to living out that future reality now."[73]

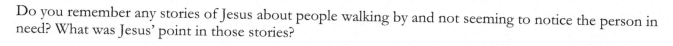

Questions for reflection:

Do you remember any stories of Jesus about people walking by and not seeming to notice the person in need? What was Jesus' point in those stories?

Teresa of Avila, a sixteenth-century Spanish mystic, wrote, "Christ has no body now on earth but yours, no hands but yours, no feet but yours. Yours are the eyes through which Christ's compassion is to look out to the world; yours are the feet with which he is to go about doing good; yours are the hands with which God is to bless people now." What thoughts does her statement arouse in you?

Prayer: *Almighty and most merciful God, we call to mind before you all whom it is easy to forget: those who are homeless, destitute, sick, isolated, and all who have no one to care for them. May we bring help and healing to those who are broken in body or spirit, that they may have comfort in sorrow, company in loneliness, and a place of safety and warmth; through Jesus Christ our Lord. Amen.*[74]

Day 6: The Worship God Wants

The Hebrew prophets often proclaimed that the people of God were missing the point. When the people adhere to the religious rituals on the outside, but on the inside are spiritually empty, when the people offer their sacrifices and observe the ritual but participate in injustice toward the poor, the prophets expose this false worship, and call the people to repentance.

In Isaiah 1, the Lord asks his people:

> *"What to me is the multitude of your sacrifices? says the LORD; I have had enough of burnt offerings of rams and the fat of fed beasts; I do not delight in the blood of bulls, or of lambs, or of goats... bringing offerings is futile; incense is an abomination to me...I cannot endure solemn assemblies with iniquity...When you stretch out your hands, I will hide my eyes from you; even though you make many prayers, I will not listen; your hands are full of blood. Wash yourselves; make yourselves clean; remove the evil of your doings from before my eyes; cease to do evil, learn to do good; seek justice, rescue the oppressed, defend the orphan, plead for the widow." (Isaiah 1:11-17)*

Almost every prophet has his version of God correcting the people about the kind of worship God wants. Frequently there is this juxtaposition of false worship and true worship. "I hate, I despise your festivals, and I take no delight in your solemn assemblies. Even though you offer me your burnt offerings and grain offerings, I will not accept them; and the offerings of well-being of your fatted animals I will not look upon. Take away from me the noise of your songs; I will not listen to the melody of your harps. But let justice roll down like waters, and righteousness like an ever-flowing stream. (Amos 5:21-24)

Through the Torah and the prophets (as well as the history, wisdom literature and Psalms) God commands God's people to care for the poor and oppressed and the powerless (the widows, orphans, and aliens), and to go beyond their care, seeking to put right the inequities that allow some to have wealth and others to be deprived of their most basic needs. To be related to God means to be committed to justice.[75] Because God is a God of justice, God's people are to be a people of justice.

Throughout their history, the people of Israel often fall back into the assumption that the worship God desires centers around rituals of sacrifices and burnt offerings; however, the prophets continually remind the people that God has no interest in external religious observances and formal temple gatherings, apart from a commitment to and concrete action on behalf of the poor and powerless. There is no mystery as to what God requires, and it has nothing to do with sacrifices and offerings. What does the Lord require? What is the worship God wants? To do justice.

"Is such the fast that I choose, a day to humble oneself? Is it to bow down the head like a bulrush, and to lie in sackcloth and ashes? Will you call this a fast, a day acceptable to the LORD? Is not this the fast that I choose: to loose the bonds of injustice, to undo the thongs of the yoke, to let the oppressed go free, and to break every yoke? Is it not to share your bread with the hungry, and bring the homeless poor into your house; when you see the naked, to cover them, and not to hide yourself from your own kin?" (Isaiah 58:5-7)

Doing justice involves repenting from one's own actions which cause others to be oppressed, and beyond that, addressing the causes of injustice, and being committed to the poor and oppressed in one's community who have no voice or power of their own by which to address the injustices against them.

The worship God wants is demonstrated by a life that expresses itself in actions for the poor and powerless, for the broken and hurting and marginalized of our world. The theologian Walter Brueggemann writes: "If our God is a God of life and love, a God who wills freedom, justice and peace for all, then we must be a people who so live…To the degree that we walk in death, hatred, oppression, violence, and injustice, or complicity thereto, the less we walk with this God that we claim to be ours."[76]   This is the fast that God desires. This is what the Lord requires. This is the worship God wants.

Questions for reflection:

How does God define worship?

What is the connection between worship and justice?

Prayer: *Grant, O God, that your holy and life-giving Spirit may move every human heart; that the barriers dividing us may crumble, suspicions disappear, and hatreds cease; and that, with our divisions healed, we might live in justice and peace; through your Son, Jesus Christ our Lord. Amen.*[77]

Taking It Further: Small Group and Chapter Summary Questions

What do you think of now when you affirm this promise of the baptismal covenant: *I promise to strive for justice in all the earth?*

How does working for social justice potentially involve one in politics?

Distinguish between social ministry and social justice, between mercy and justice.

What role does the church play in advancing God's kingdom?

Why do justice issues seem less apparent in the suburbs than they do in the city?

Why might the church be tempted to avoid working for social justice?.

Why do you or do you not participate in a community partnership for justice (such as IMPACT in Charlottesville)?

Shane Claiborne makes this statement: "What the world needs is people who believe so much in another world that they cannot help but begin enacting it now."[78] What do you think he means?

Which of the Bible readings took on a new meaning for you this week?

What questions or issues do you want to discuss further with others?

What do you want to remember from this chapter?

Recommended resources for further study:

Annan, *Following Jesus Through the Eye of the Needle: Living Fully, Loving Dangerously*

Brueggemann, T*o Act Justly, Love Tenderly, Walk Humbly*

Claiborne, *The Irresistible Revolution: Living As an Ordinary Radical*

Myers, *The Biblical Vision of Sabbath Economics*

Samson, *Justice in the Burbs: Being the Hands of Jesus Wherever You Live*

Wallis, *God's Politics: Why the Right Gets It Wrong and the Left Doesn't Get It*

Chapter Eight: Striving for Peace in All the Earth

Do you intend to continue in the covenant God made with you in holy baptism:
to live among God's faithful people,
to hear the word of God and share in the Lord's supper,
to proclaim the good news of God in Christ through word and deed,
to serve all people, following the example of Jesus,
and to strive for justice and peace in all the earth?"

WE CONCLUDE OUR STUDY of the baptismal covenant with the final promise, striving for peace in all the earth. Another way to proclaim the good news of God in Christ in words and deeds is speaking for and working for peace in our community and in our world. Peace is one of the deepest longings of the human heart. Whether you call it harmony, serenity, or wholeness, "the yearning for it exists somewhere in every human being."[79] As we move through the days of this week, we will study six steps of peace.

Day 1: Peace begins with God.

Psalm 85   LORD, you were favorable to your land; you restored the fortunes of Jacob. ² You forgave the iniquity of your people; you pardoned all their sin. ³ You withdrew all your wrath; you turned from your hot anger. ⁴ Restore us again, O God of our salvation, and put away your indignation toward us. ⁵ Will you be angry with us forever? Will you prolong your anger to all generations? ⁶ Will you not revive us again, so that your people may rejoice in you? ⁷ Show us your steadfast love, O LORD, and grant us your salvation. ⁸ Let me hear what God the LORD will speak, for he will speak peace to his people, to his faithful, to those who turn to him in their hearts. ⁹ Surely his salvation is at hand for those who fear him, that his glory may dwell in our land. ¹⁰ Steadfast love and faithfulness will meet; righteousness and peace will kiss each other. ¹¹ Faithfulness will spring up from the ground, and righteousness will look down from the sky. ¹² The LORD will give what is good, and our land will yield its increase. ¹³ Righteousness will go before him, and will make a path for his steps.

In the Old Testament, the Hebrew word for peace is *shalom*. *Shalom* means the absence of war and conflict, but it also means friendship, contentment, security, health, abundance, tranquility, and harmony with nature. "And it means these things for everyone, not only a select few. *Shalom* is ultimately a blessing, a gift from God. It is not a human endeavor."[80]

In the New Testament, Jesus inaugurates the kingdom of God, which is the kingdom of shalom. He brings good news to the poor, proclaims release to the captives and oppressed, and recovery of sight to the blind. (Luke 4:18) Through the life of Jesus, God intends to restore shalom to his creation.

The apostle Paul uses the word "peace" to describe the reconciled relationship between God and God's people (Ephesians 2:11-22). When we receive the grace, love, and forgiveness of God into our lives, we receive the Spirit of Jesus Christ, which brings us peace. Paul even says that Jesus Christ *is* our peace. But this peace is much more than a personal peace of heart or peace of mind. Peace with God leads to peace with others. Peace with God is the foundation of all other relationships.

Question for reflection:

If peace is a gift from God, how is it that we are also to strive for it?

Prayer: *Jesus, my life was in chaos until you entered it. Thank you for the forgiveness that brought me peace. Deepen my sense of your presence by keeping me close to you. Teach me to become a peacemaker—loving justice, doing right, and leading others along the path of peace.*[81]

Day 2: Peace in Christ

> **Romans 12:17-18** *Do not repay anyone evil for evil, but take thought for what is noble in the sight of all.* ^{18} *If it is possible, so far as it depends on you, live peaceably with all.*

"Like the Hebrew concept of *shalom*, the New Testament portrays peace as much more than the absence of conflict. Mark's Gospel, for instance, links healing and peace by capturing Jesus' words to a woman he has just healed. He tells her to 'go in peace' (Mark 5:34). The New Testament further develops our understanding of peace by revealing Jesus as the source of all peace. Though we were alienated from God because of our sins, Jesus reconciled us, making peace through his blood. Peace with God produces peace with others and peace within ourselves. When Christ's kingdom is fully established, all strife will cease, and those who belong to him will enjoy forever the fullness of peace – health, wholeness, well-being, tranquility, satisfaction, safety, prosperity, and perfect contentment."[82]

If the first step of peace is God's step toward us, the second step of peace is the step toward our brothers and sisters in Christ. The Apostle Paul instructs the Christians in Rome to live peacefully with each other: "Let love be genuine...love one another with mutual affection... outdo one another in showing honor... Rejoice in hope, be patient in suffering, persevere in prayer... ... Live in harmony with one another" (Romans 12).

The peace of God leads us to be peacemakers first of all with our brothers and sisters in Christ. Jesus teaches that there is a link between our relationship with God, and our relationships with other people. If we love God then we will love others. If we are forgiven by God, then we will be forgiving of others. And when he interprets the fifth commandment, You shall not murder, he gives it a much more radical, personal interpretation: "if you are angry with a brother or sister, you will be liable to judgment; and if you insult a brother or sister, you will be liable to the council; and if you say, 'You fool,' you will be liable to the hell of fire. So when you are offering your gift at the altar, if you remember that your brother or sister has something against you, leave your gift there before the altar and go; first be reconciled to your brother or sister, and then come and offer your gift" (Matthew 5:21-24).

This is the meaning behind the Sharing of the Peace in the worship service. It is intended to be much more than a "hello, how are you?" moment. It is a sign that we open ourselves to the healing and reconciling power of God's love and offer ourselves to be agents of that love with each other and in the world.[83]

Is there anything currently going on within your congregation that requires peacemaking? Has a lack of respect been demonstrated or an insult given? There will be relationship issues and hurt feelings in every congregation. The key is whether people have the humility and spiritual maturity to work for forgiveness, reconciliation, and peace. "So when you are offering your gift at the altar, if you remember that your brother or sister has something against you, leave your gift there before the altar and go; first be reconciled to your brother or sister, and then come and offer your gift."

Questions for reflection:

In the passage mentioned above (Matthew 5:21-24), what connection is Jesus drawing between insulting another and killing another?

What is the foundation for relationships between Christians?

Prayer: *O God, it is your will to hold both heaven and earth in a single peace. Let the design of your great love shine on the waste of our wraths and sorrows, and give peace to your church, peace among nations, peace in our homes, and peace in our hearts; through your Son, Jesus Christ our Lord. Amen.*[84]

Day 3: Peace in the World

2 Corinthians 5:16-20 From now on, therefore, we regard no one from a human point of view; even though we once knew Christ from a human point of view, we know him no longer in that way. [17] So if anyone is in Christ, there is a new creation: everything old has passed away; see, everything has become new! [18] All this is from God, who reconciled us to himself through Christ, and has given us the ministry of reconciliation; [19] that is, in Christ God was reconciling the world to himself, not counting their trespasses against them, and entrusting the message of reconciliation to us. [20] So we are ambassadors for Christ, since God is making his appeal through us; we entreat you on behalf of Christ, be reconciled to God.

The third step of peace leads us into the world. As God's peacemakers, we are called to strive for peace and justice in all the earth. We are called to be peacemakers in the world, and to stand especially with those who have no power and no voice. We are to live out a connectedness to the least, the last, and the lost.

In Jesus Christ we have been given the ministry of reconciliation (2 Cor. 5:18). We are called to build bridges to other people. When people from our church go and prepare and serve the dinner and sit with the homeless people at the Salvation Army, we are building a bridge. When we invite the homeless women to stay at our church for two weeks in the winter, when we support other churches and ministries in Togo, Honduras, or India, we are building bridges. As we minister with the people in southwest Virginia, we are building a bridge. Through the church, God desires to build bridges of peace.

"Blessed are the peacemakers, Jesus said, for they will be called the children of God" (Matthew 5:9).

One day a man with a serious drinking problem dropped in to talk with Virgil Vogt, one of the elders of Reba Place Fellowship in Evanston, Illinois. When Virgil invited him to accept Jesus Christ and join the community of believers, the man insisted that he simply wanted money for a bus ticket to Cleveland.

"Okay," Virgil agreed, "we can give you that kind of help too, if that's all you really want."

He was quiet a moment, then he shook his head.

"You know something?" he said, looking straight at the man. "You've just really let me off the hook. Because if you had chosen a new way of life in the kingdom of God, then as your brother I would have had to lay down my whole life for you. This house, my time, all my money, whatever you needed to meet your needs would have been totally at your disposal for the rest of your life. But all you want is some money for a bus ticket…"

The man was so startled he stood up and left, forgetting to take the money. But on Sunday he was back, this time sitting next to Virgil in the worship service.[85]

Questions for reflection:

What bridges need to be built in your community?

What bridges need to be built in the world?

Prayer: *Draw your church together, O God, into one great company of disciples, together following our teacher Jesus Christ into every walk of life, together serving in Christ's mission to the world, and together witnessing to your love wherever you will send us.*[86]

Day 4: Peace with Enemies

Matthew 5:38-48 *"You have heard that it was said, 'An eye for an eye and a tooth for a tooth.' [39] But I say to you, Do not resist an evildoer. But if anyone strikes you on the right cheek, turn the other also; [40] and if anyone wants to sue you and take your coat, give your cloak as well; [41] and if anyone forces you to go one mile, go also the second mile. [42] Give to everyone who begs from you, and do not refuse anyone who wants to borrow from you. [43] "You have heard that it was said, 'You shall love your neighbor and hate your enemy.' [44] But I say to you, Love your enemies and pray for those who persecute you, [45] so that you may be children of your Father in heaven; for he makes his sun rise on the evil and on the good, and sends rain on the righteous and on the unrighteous. [46] For if you love those who love you, what reward do you have? Do not even the tax collectors do the same? [47]And if you greet only your brothers and sisters, what more are you doing than others? Do not even the Gentiles do the same? [48] Be perfect, therefore, as your heavenly Father is perfect."*

The fourth step of peace is to be peacemakers even toward our enemies. Once again from Romans 12, listen to the words of Paul: "Bless those who persecute you; bless and do not curse them… Do not repay anyone evil for evil…If it is possible, so far as it depends on you, live peaceably with all…if your enemies are hungry, feed them; if they are thirsty, give them something to drink; (for by doing this you will heap burning coals on their heads.) Do not be overcome by evil, but overcome evil with good."

We are not to return evil with evil, or take revenge, or treat our enemy as an enemy. When we repay evil for evil, we actually become the very ones that we despise. Jesus teaches his followers to love their enemies, and to bless those who are against them. This is the hardest step of peace, to be good to those who are not good to you. As with all the steps of peace, this one requires God's grace working in and through us. When it happens, that is, when a sense of shalom exists between our "enemies" and ourselves, it is a demonstration of the in-breaking of God's kingdom among us.

Questions for reflection:

How can you break the cycle of revenge and retaliation?

What happens if in trying to treat your enemy with respect and peace, you are taken advantage of?

What "enemies" do you need to pray for?

Prayer: *Gracious and holy God, lead us from death to life, from falsehood to truth. Lead us from despair to hope, from fear to trust. Lead us from hate to love, from war to peace. Let peace fill our hearts, our world, our universe; through Jesus Christ, our Savior and Lord. Amen.*[87]

Day 5: Peace with Creation

Isaiah 11:6-9 *The wolf shall live with the lamb, the leopard shall lie down with the kid, the calf and the lion and the fatling together, and a little child shall lead them.* [7] *The cow and the bear shall graze, their young shall lie down together; and the lion shall eat straw like the ox.* [8] *The nursing child shall play over the hole of the asp, and the weaned child shall put its hand on the adder's den.* [9] *They will not hurt or destroy on all my holy mountain; for the earth will be full of the knowledge of the LORD as the waters cover the sea.*

The fifth step of peace is to see our connectedness to God's creation. The Bible says that all creation groans to be restored into the harmony God intended for it (Romans 8:18-23). The prophet Isaiah voices the dream of God's creation of a peaceable kingdom where the lion would dwell with the lamb, (and where people would refashion their swords into plows).

We suburban North Americans often forget our relationship to the rest of God's creation. We are sufficiently removed from the land. But there are times when we can see our connection more clearly. Times when we feel at one with nature, times when we know we are very much interrelated with the rest of creation.

Questions for reflection:

Where in nature do you experience the peace of connectedness to God's creation?

What can you do to help move Isaiah's vision from a dream to reality?

Prayer: *Almighty God, in giving us dominion over things on earth, you made us coworkers in your creation. Give us wisdom and reverence to use the resources of nature so that no one may suffer from our abuse of them, and that generations yet to come may continue to praise you for your bounty; through your Son, Jesus Christ our Lord. Amen.*[88]

Day 6: The Friends of Peace

> *Galatians 5:22-23   By contrast, the fruit of the Spirit is love, joy, peace, patience, kindness, generosity, faithfulness,* [23] *gentleness, and self-control. There is no law against such things.*

The sixth step of peace is that peace always exists with other realities. Peace is rarely mentioned in the Bible by itself. It is usually mentioned in relationship with other qualities. For example, in Colossians 3, "As God's chosen ones, holy and beloved, clothe yourselves with compassion, kindness, humility, meekness, and patience. Bear with one another and, if anyone has a complaint against another, forgive each other... Above all, clothe yourselves with love, which binds everything together in perfect harmony. And let the peace of Christ rule in your hearts, to which indeed you were called in the one body."

In Galatians 5, Paul mentions peace as part of the work of the Holy Spirit in the life of a Christian: "the fruit of the Spirit is love, joy, peace, patience, kindness, generosity, faithfulness, gentleness, and self-control."

And in Philippians 4, Paul writes "Rejoice in the Lord always... Let your gentleness be known to everyone...Do not worry about anything, but in everything by prayer and supplication with thanksgiving let your requests be made known to God. And the peace of God, which surpasses all understanding, will guard your hearts and your minds in Christ Jesus."

You have likely seen the bumper-sticker, "If you want peace, work for justice." Peace is dependent on the existence of other realities. Peace with other Christians, striving for peace in the world, peace with our enemies, and peace with God's creation. The peace of God leads to all these other experiences of peace.

Peace Prayer of St. Francis

Lord, make me an instrument of Your peace.
Where there is hatred, let me sow love;
where there is injury, pardon;
where there is doubt, faith;
where there is despair, hope;
where there is darkness, light;
where there is sadness, joy.
O, Divine Master,
grant that I may not so much seek to be consoled as to console;
to be understood as to understand;
to be loved as to love;
for it is in giving that we receive;
it is in pardoning that we are pardoned;
it is in dying that we are born again to eternal life. Amen.

(Tom Czelusta): Saint Francis was born in Assisi, Italy in 1182. He lived and preached a life of poverty and love of God. His "Peace Prayer" is a call to action – a "peace plan" – for each of us. We do not need a Geneva Convention or a Camp David Accord, as good as they might be, to be peace-makers. Each of us has a "peace plan" right here – right now – bringing light where there is darkness, joy where there is sadness, hope where there is despair, love where there is hatred, and faith where there is doubt.

Questions for reflection:

According to the prayer attributed to St. Francis, what helps to bring about peace?

Who is working for peace in your community?

How can you support and affirm their work?

Taking It Further: Small Group and Chapter Summary Questions

What examples from Jesus' life demonstrate peace-making?

On which of the 6 steps of peace would you like to concentrate?

The early Christian Church developed a step-by-step process for dealing with conflicts between people (Matthew 18:15-17). "If another member of the church sins against you, go and point out the fault when the two of you are alone. If the member listens to you, you have regained that one. [16] But if you are not listened to, take one or two others along with you, so that every word may be confirmed by the evidence of two or three witnesses. [17] If the member refuses to listen to them, tell it to the church; and if the offender refuses to listen even to the church, let such a one be to you as a Gentile and a tax collector." What guidance do you draw from this peace-making process?

What do you think of now when you affirm this promise of the baptismal covenant: *I promise to strive for peace in all the earth?*

What reactions and thoughts do you have about these statements about peace?

All works of love are works of peace. (Mother Theresa)

Common folk, not statesmen, nor generals nor great men of affairs, but just simple plain men and women, can do something to build a better, peaceful world. The future hope of peace lies with such personal .... service. (Henry Cadbury, accepting the Nobel Peace Prize)

Peace between countries must rest on the solid foundation of love between individuals. (Mahatma Gandhi)

We have an extraordinary God. God is a mighty God, but this God needs you. When someone is hungry, bread doesn't come down from heaven. When God wants to feed the hungry, you and I must feed the hungry. And now God wants peace in the world. (Archbishop Desmond Tutu)

If there is to be peace in the world,
There must be peace in the nations.
If there is to be peace in the nations,
There must be peace in the cities.
If there is to be peace in the cities,
There must be peace between neighbors.
If there is to be peace between neighbors,
There must be peace in the home.
If there is to be peace in the home,
There must be peace in the heart. (Lao Tzu)

We, the peoples of the United Nations, determined to save succeeding generations from the scourge of war, which twice in our lifetime has brought untold sorrow to mankind, and to reaffirm faith in fundamental human rights, in the dignity and worth of the human person, in the equal right of men and women and of nations large and small....And for these ends to practice tolerance and live together in peace with one another as good neighbors...have resolved to combine our efforts to accomplish these aims. (Preamble, Charter of the United Nations.)

True peace is not merely the absence of tension: It is the presence of justice. (Martin Luther King, Jr.)

We must come to see that peace is not merely a distant goal that we seek, but a means by which we arrive at that goal. (Martin Luther King, Jr)

Which of the Bible readings took on a new meaning for you this week?

What questions or issues do you want to discuss further with others?

What do you want to remember from this chapter?

Recommended resources for further study:

Arnold, *Seeking Peace: Notes and Conversations Along the Way*

Tutu, *No Future Without Forgiveness*

Chapter Nine: Practicing the Faith

Pastor: "You have made public profession of your faith. Do you intend to continue in the covenant God made with you in holy baptism:
to live among God's faithful people,
to hear the word of God and share in the Lord's supper,
to proclaim the good news of God in Christ through word and deed,
to serve all people, following the example of Jesus,
and to strive for justice and peace in all the earth?"

Those affirming their baptism: "I do and I ask God to help and guide me."[89]

AS WE LIVE OUT OUR BAPTISM, we are drawn into the way of Jesus. As we live into the gifts and promises of our baptismal covenant, the Holy Spirit equips us to be the Body of Christ wherever we go. As we live with God's faithful people, as we hear the Word and share in the Lord's Supper, as we proclaim the good news through word and deed, as we serve all people, following the example of Jesus, and as we strive for justice and peace in all the earth, we practice the faith.

Day 1: Growing/Making Disciples

Matthew 28:18-20 And Jesus came and said to them, "All authority in heaven and on earth has been given to me. ¹⁹ Go therefore and make disciples of all nations, baptizing them in the name of the Father and of the Son and of the Holy Spirit, ²⁰ and teaching them to obey everything that I have commanded you. And remember, I am with you always, to the end of the age."

After the resurrection, Jesus gives his mission to his disciples, commissioning them to go and make disciples. As they go into the world, they are to invite other people into the journey of following Jesus. And how are they (and we) to do this? By baptizing people, that is, by joining them to the grace of God and the community of Christ. By teaching them the way of Jesus (by teaching and living and modeling the way of Jesus in our lives, and teaching and living by his kingdom values). And one more thing: by remembering that Jesus is always with us, and that it is he who empowers us and makes disciples. (We rely on his power and authority.)

Our mission is to be disciples of Jesus and make disciples of Jesus. To assist people in their walk with God so that they move from where they are to where God wants them to be — toward spiritual maturity. (Ephesians 4:11-13. "The gifts he gave were that some would be apostles, some prophets, some evangelists, some pastors and teachers, to equip the saints for the work of ministry, for building up the body of Christ, until all of us come to the unity of the faith and of the knowledge of the Son of God, to maturity, to the measure of the full stature of Christ.")

In his letters, the apostle Paul uses language like Christ being formed in us, or having the mind of Christ, or being made complete in Christ, or growing up in Christ, or being made holy or sanctified, or being transformed into his likeness. It is the Holy Spirit who transforms us into the life and character of Christ.

Questions for reflection:

What primary teachings do you think Jesus is referring to in Matthew 28:20 ("teaching them to obey everything that I have commanded you.")?

What does it mean to you to "practice the faith?"

Pray the prayer from the *Affirmation of Baptism* service as your own prayer:

Father in heaven, for Jesus' sake, stir up in me the gift of your Holy Spirit; confirm my faith, guide my life, empower me in my serving, give me patience in suffering, and bring me to everlasting life. Amen.

Day 2: Learning Christ

Ephesians 4:17-24 Now this I affirm and insist on in the Lord: you must no longer live as the Gentiles live, in the futility of their minds. [18] They are darkened in their understanding, alienated from the life of God because of their ignorance and hardness of heart. [19] They have lost all sensitivity and have abandoned themselves to licentiousness, greedy to practice every kind of impurity. [20] That is not the way you learned Christ! [21] For surely you have heard about him and were taught in him, as truth is in Jesus. [22] You were taught to put away your former way of life, your old self, corrupt and deluded by its lusts, [23] and to be renewed in the spirit of your minds, [24] and to clothe yourselves with the new self, created according to the likeness of God in true righteousness and holiness.

Learning Christ. That phrase comes from Ephesians 4. In this part of the letter, the author is encouraging Christians in Ephesus to set aside their old ways of living apart from Christ, and to put on the new nature of Jesus Christ. He uses the phrase "learning Christ." What is meant by that phrase?

In one sense it means learning *about* Jesus Christ. And that's certainly part of what we do in our discipleship ministries with children, youth and adults. We learn about Jesus Christ through the Bible. In the gospels, we learn that Jesus said and did some very radical things. He forgave sins. He said that he and God the Father were one; He said that if you've seen me you've seen the Father. Jesus said, "I am the way and the truth and the life." He calls himself the son of man, and the gospel writers call him the son of God and the Word of God. Other New Testament writers call him the Alpha and the Omega, the beginning and the end. They claim that in him all things in the world hold together. They point to his death on the cross and the resurrection as the event through which God has restored the world unto himself.

In one sense, learning Christ means learning *about* this unique person. But in another sense, *learning Christ* refers to a way of life, a new nature, Jesus Christ himself being formed in us by the Holy Spirit. This is the sense of *learning Christ* that we want for our congregations, and for all on this journey with Jesus. We pray that our entire lives will be a journey with Jesus. A life of learning, growing, trusting, and loving. A journey that will never end. Even more important than learning about Jesus is to learn Jesus. To live Jesus. To learn by the Spirit to live Christ. To learn to allow Jesus Christ to live in us and through us. Because "no one who meets Jesus ever stays the same."[90]

Questions for reflection:

In what ways are you *learning Christ?*

In what ways are you *living Christ?*

Pray the prayer from the *Affirmation of Baptism* service as your own prayer:

Father in heaven, for Jesus' sake, stir up in me the gift of your Holy Spirit; confirm my faith, guide my life, empower me in my serving, give me patience in suffering, and bring me to everlasting life. Amen.

Day 3: God at Work in Us

> *Philippians 2:12-13* *Therefore, my beloved, just as you have always obeyed me, not only in my presence, but much more now in my absence, work out your own salvation with fear and trembling;* [13] *for it is God who is at work in you, enabling you both to will and to work for his good pleasure.*

Dwight Moody was asked why he regularly prays that he might be filled with God's Holy Spirit. He responded, "Because I leak." Martin Luther taught people to return to their baptism every day and wear it as their daily garment: to put off the old life and put on the new life of Christ.

From baptism throughout our journey, the Lord feeds us and nourishes us, teaches us and talks with us so that we will turn toward him more and more and become like him more and more. When God is working in our lives, we will see an increase of generosity, gratitude and joy; an increasing communication in prayer, and an increasing dependence and trust in God. Through the work of God, we are being renewed, transformed, changed.

When Richard Foster attempts to explain how God transforms us through the work of the Holy Spirit, he refers to the "principle of indirection." "We cannot by direct effort make ourselves into the kind of people who can live fully alive to God. Only God can accomplish this in us. Only God can incline our heart toward him. Only God can reprogram the deeply ingrained habit patterns of sin that constantly predispose us toward evil and transform them into even more deeply ingrained habit patters of 'righteousness and peace and joy in the Holy Spirit' (Rom.14:17). And God freely and graciously invites us to participate in this transforming process. But not on our own."[91]

Discipleship is an ongoing relationship, an ongoing work of God's transformation. May we be transformed, continually, so that we may be useful for God.

Questions for reflection:

When it comes to our spiritual growth, what do you think Foster means by the word, "indirection?"

What connections do you see between the words of Moody ("I leak") and Luther's concept of returning to our baptism daily?

Pray the prayer from the *Affirmation of Baptism* service, once again, as your own prayer:

Father in heaven, for Jesus' sake, stir up in me the gift of your Holy Spirit; confirm my faith, guide my life, empower me in my serving, give me patience in suffering, and bring me to everlasting life. Amen.

Day 4: Sitting at the Feet of Jesus

Luke 10:38-42 Now as they went on their way, he entered a certain village, where a woman named Martha welcomed him into her home. 39 She had a sister named Mary, who sat at the Lord's feet and listened to what he was saying. 40 But Martha was distracted by her many tasks; so she came to him and asked, "Lord, do you not care that my sister has left me to do all the work by myself? Tell her then to help me." 41 But the Lord answered her, "Martha, Martha, you are worried and distracted by many things; 42 there is need of only one thing. Mary has chosen the better part, which will not be taken away from her."

In his book, *The Heart of Christianity*, Marcus Borg asks the question, what does it mean to love God above all else, to love God with our whole lives? And then he answers his own question: "Loving God means paying attention to God and to what God loves. The way we do this is through 'practice.'"[92] By "practice" he means all the things that Christians do together and individually as a way of paying attention to God. They include being part of a Christian church, and taking part in its life together and being nourished by that community. Things like worship, Christian formation, prayer and spending time with the Bible. Borg also mentions loving what God loves through the practice of hospitality, compassion and justice in the world.[93]

We have a similar list of faith practices on our sanctuary walls that we adapted from Glenn McDonald's marks of a disciple: a heart for Christ alone, a mind transformed by the Word, arms of love, knees for prayer, a voice to speak the good news, and feet of a servant.[94] These are not to be understood as lists of chores to be done. They are not a list of requirements to be completed. These spiritual disciplines are God's gift to us that allow us to "place ourselves before God" so that God can transform us.[95] They help us develop a love for God and a readiness to serve God in God's world. They are tools the Holy Spirit uses to form the character of Christ in us.

Jesus told Martha that only one thing is needed (and Mary has chosen what is better). The one thing is being in the presence of Jesus. "And placing ourselves there is a choice. Aligning ourselves with his thoughts, his desires, and his grace is not a matter of temperament or DNA. In the end it must be a lifelong, sustainable decision. The *Godward* practices of Christian spirituality keep us at the Lord's feet, listening to what he is saying."[96] In practicing the faith, we take up a way of life that helps us pay attention to God.

"The marks of discipleship have nothing to do with a legalistic, law-oriented approach to Christian faith. The purpose is not to create super Christians or any kind of spiritual elite. No one earns salvation or gains any special favor from God by practicing the marks. They are simply habits of the soul that open us to the wonder and mystery of God's active presence in our lives. They keep us focused; they fix our attention on the things of God."[97]

Questions for reflection:

Summarize Jesus' message to Martha:

What is the purpose of spiritual disciplines?

Day 5: Marks of Discipleship

Acts 2:42 They devoted themselves to the apostles' teaching and fellowship, to the breaking of bread and the prayers.

2 Peter 3:18 But grow in the grace and knowledge of our Lord and Savior Jesus Christ. To him be the glory both now and to the day of eternity. Amen.

Several years ago, The ELCA presented seven important faith practices: praying, studying, worshiping, inviting, encouraging, serving, and giving. They describe both the lives of individual Christians as well as the essential activities of the church itself. Michael Foss and Glenn McDonald offer similar lists. Our vocation is to be followers of Jesus in every circle of our lives: to have a heart for Jesus Christ above all else; a mind transformed by the Word; arms of love; knees for prayer; a voice to speak the good news; and feet of a servant. With each faith practice connected to a body part, even the children can understand the vocation of a Christian in God's world. Consider these six characteristics of a growing disciple of Jesus:

A heart for Christ alone.

This is the most important characteristic. Jesus makes it clear that our fidelity to him is prior and superior to every other relationship or aspiration life has to offer.[98]

A mind transformed by the Word.

To have a mind transformed by the Word we have to immerse ourselves in the Word of God. We read the Bible not just for information, but for transformation, so that we not only read and listen, but we also pray it, breathe it and live it.[99]

Arms of love.

We love other people because God has poured his love into our hearts. We change others and we ourselves are changed through sharing God's love.[100] We grow in our faith when we are in small group relationships with other people of faith.

Knees for prayer.

We are most available for God's Spirit to work in and through our lives when prayer is central in our lives. Prayer is about joining our hearts with the heart of God.[101]

A voice to speak the good news.

Being a witness for Jesus Christ involves a process of listening, hearing, speaking, praying, and encouraging others. Jesus calls us to share our hope and our lives with other people.[102]

The feet of a servant.

We are blessed by God to be a blessing to others. We "go in Christ" to serve other people. The faith practices or spiritual disciplines have no merit in and of themselves. "Their purpose—their only purpose—is to place us before God...Then the grace of God steps in and takes this simple offering of ourselves and creates out of it the kind of person who embodies the goodness of God."[103] Of course, even the desire to live for God, and to be in God's presence, comes from the grace of God. But we are not meant to be passive. There are things for us to do that put us in a place for the Spirit to grow us in Christ.

The following chart offers a comparison of four separate yet similar lists of faith practices.

Faith Practices

A Heart for Christ Alone	Share in the Lord's supper	Worship	Weekly Worship
A Mind Transformed by the Word	Hear the word of God	Study	Bible Reading
Arms of Love	Live among God's faithful people	Encourage	Spiritual Friendships
Knees for Prayer		Pray	Daily Prayer
A Voice to Speak the Good News	Proclaim the good news of God in Christ through word and deed	Invite	
A Spirit of Servanthood and Stewardship	Serve all people, following the example of Jesus	Serve, Give	Service, Giving
	Strive for justice and peace		
The Disciple Making Church by Glenn McDonald	*Evangelical Lutheran Worship* (Affirmation of Baptism)	*Seven Faith Practices* @ www.elca.org	*Power Surge* by Michael Foss

Questions for reflection:

What observations do you make as you compare the lists of faith practices?

On which spiritual discipline or faith practice do you need to focus? Make it a matter of your prayer.

On which practice do you think your congregation most needs to focus?

Day 6: I Do and I Ask God to Help and Guide Me

> ***Romans 6:3-5*** *Do you not know that all of us who have been baptized into Christ Jesus were baptized into his death?* [4] *Therefore we have been buried with him by baptism into death, so that, just as Christ was raised from the dead by the glory of the Father, so we too might walk in newness of life.* [5] *For if we have been united with him in a death like his, we will certainly be united with him in a resurrection like his.*

We conclude our study of the baptismal covenant with the *Affirmation of Baptism* service:

Affirmation of Baptism

The leader addresses the people.

Do you desire to affirm your baptism?

The people respond.

I do.

Do you renounce the devil and all the forces that defy God?

I renounce them.

Do you renounce the powers of this world that rebel against God?

I renounce them.

Do you renounce the ways of sin that draw you from God?

I renounce them.

Do you believe in God the Father?

I believe.

Do you believe in Jesus Christ, the Son of God?

I believe.

Do you believe in God the Holy Spirit?

I believe.

Do you intend to continue in the covenant God made with you in holy baptism:
    to live among God's faithful people,
    to hear the word of God and share in the Lord's supper,
    to proclaim the good news of God in Christ through word and deed,
    to serve all people, following the example of Jesus,
    and to strive for justice and peace in all the earth?

I do, and I ask God to help and guide me.[104]

The five promises of the baptismal covenant provide a thorough outline of life within the faith community as well as the baptismal vocation in the world. Taken together, the five promises describe the recurring rhythm of being nurtured by God's gifts for God's mission in the world. And, unlike many other lists of faith practices or spiritual disciplines, they include within the baptismal vocation God's call to stand for and work for justice and peace in the world. Finally, the response of the disciple, "I do, and I ask God to help and guide me," acknowledges the reliance upon God's gracious Spirit in shaping disciples, forming the church, calling them into God's mission, and strengthening them for God's mission.

When we affirm our baptism, we say "Yes" to the God who has said "Yes" to us even before we were born.

Questions for reflection:

What connections do you see in the language of baptism as death and resurrection (Romans 6:3-5) and the litany for affirmation of baptism?

What reassurance do you find in the concluding response to the fivefold question of the baptismal covenant: *I do, and I ask God to help and guide me?*

Pray the prayer from the *Affirmation of Baptism* service, once again, as your own prayer:

Father in heaven, for Jesus' sake, stir up in me the gift of your Holy Spirit; confirm my faith, guide my life, empower me in my serving, give me patience in suffering, and bring me to everlasting life. Amen.

Taking It Further: Small Group and Chapter Summary Questions

The baptismal covenant seems to be one of the most under-utilized summaries of the Christian life. What have you learned about it that you would like to remember?

Do you see any difference between the words "disciple" and "Christian?" Do you think there should be any differences between them?

How might faith practices or spiritual disciplines take on the wrong emphasis of "works righteousness?"

What are some of the promises of God in baptism?

What is the relationship of confirmation to baptism? How do they fit together in the life of a Christian?

What promises are made or what promises did you make when you were confirmed?

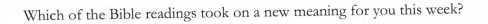

Which of the Bible readings took on a new meaning for you this week?

What questions or issues do you want to discuss further with others?

Use the Affirmation of Baptism service (Day 6) in your group time this week.

Do an online search for the hymn by John Bell, *Will You Come and Follow Me.* It is a beautiful invitation from Jesus to a potential follower. And in the final stanza, the follower responds. Use the hymn to center your reflections as you conclude this study of the baptismal covenant. How do you respond to the questions Jesus asks you in the hymn?

Recommended resources for further study:

Foss, *Power Surge: Six Marks of Discipleship for a Changing Church*

Foster, *Celebration of Discipline: The Path to Spiritual Growth*

Foster, *Life with God: Reading the Bible for Spiritual Transformation*

Jones, *Traveling Together: A Guide for Disciple-Forming Congregations*

McDonald, *The Disciple Making Church: From Dry Bones to Spiritual Vitality*

Willard, *The Great Omission: Reclaiming Jesus' Essential Teachings on Discipleship*

Chapter Ten: Next Steps...

Possible Uses

HOW MIGHT THIS RESOURCE be used by groups?

as the curriculum for new or ongoing small groups;

as the curriculum for discipleship groups (groups of 3 or 4 who meet together weekly to walk with each other in the faith);

as the curriculum for a new member class, baptismal class, or a catechumenate group, learning about the life of a disciple;

as the curriculum for a confirmation class for an in-depth study of what it means to affirm one's baptism;

as group devotional material for church councils and other groups;

as the curriculum for Sunday morning adult forums;

as a resource for a worship series about baptism, spiritual formation, or discipleship.

A Worship Resource

Pastors and worship planning teams may choose to use this resource in planning a congregational study of the life commitments of the *Affirmation of Baptism*. There are a few strategic liturgical days on which to begin or conclude this study: Baptism of our Lord, Easter, Pentecost, Reformation, and All Saints. Here is a possible seven week schedule, building toward a congregation-wide Affirmation of Baptism:

Week One: *Come to the Water* (Chapter 1)

Week Two: *Living Among God's Faithful People* (Chapter 2)

Week Three: *Hearing the Word of God and Sharing in the Lord's Supper* (Chapters 3 & 4)

Week Four: *Proclaiming the Good News through Words and Deeds* (Chapter 5)

Week Five: *Serving All People* (Chapter 6)

Week Six: *Striving for Justice and Peace in All the Earth* (Chapters 7 & 8)

Week Seven: *Practicing the Faith* (Chapter 9); Affirmation of Baptism

The series could also be shortened into a 5-week series, such as a midweek Lenten study, omitting weeks one and seven above.

The Rest of the *Going Deeper* Series

Perhaps you (and your group) would like to continue your study of what it means to follow Jesus? Consider one of the other books of the series, *Going Deeper: A Journey with Jesus*. These five books provide a variety of discipleship studies for small groups and individuals. The books can also be used as curriculum for adult forums and high school Sunday School classes, resources for special worship series, and study guides for church leadership development. Although the sequence of the books is intentional, each book is self-contained and can be used independently from the other books.

Yearning for God (Book One) begins with the human yearning of the creature to know the Creator, and it progresses through several life-changing encounters of people with Jesus Christ. Encountering Christ speaks to the heart as nothing else can do.

God Comes to Us (Book Two) Having encountered Christ (in book one), we desire to learn more about God. This volume makes use of the creeds to introduce the fullness of God as Father, Son, and Holy Spirit, a God who wants to be in relationship with his people.

The Fruit of the Spirit (Book Four) studies the fruit of the Spirit, the qualities—the character of Jesus Christ—that the Spirit desires to produce in the church and in individual disciples.

The Body of Christ (Book Five) studies the biblical images of church to present a picture of what it means to be the church today, living among God's people, and sent out into the world. This resource also offers a 12-month set of devotions on leadership for church councils.

Chapter Eleven: Small Group Guidelines

This series, *Going Deeper: A Journey with Jesus,* is intended to be a readily accessible resource for small group use. It does not require a leader's guide, nor extra preparation for small group leaders. For small groups that already have designated leaders, the leaders can facilitate the discussion. Other small groups will be able to use this resource with a shared or a rotational leadership. If you are using this discipleship resource in a small group, please review this chapter as a group at the beginning of your time together.

A good way to begin is to form a small group that agrees to meet together for about 10-12 weeks. This approach assumes that the group will complete almost one chapter a week. The group will then have the option of deciding to continue with another study for another 10-12 more weeks.

If you are meeting with your small group each week, consider the group meeting day as the seventh day of the week (that is, begin Day 1 on the day after your small group meeting day).

At the end of each chapter is a section entitled: "Taking It Further: Small Group and Chapter Summary Questions." I suggest that small groups begin their discussions with these summary questions. The group can use any or all of these questions, and any questions in the chapter which the participants want to discuss. Of course, the group members will also have some of their own questions and issues. I advise that groups not feel the need to begin with Day 1 and move methodically through the seven days of the chapter, attempting to address each question. Be flexible with the curriculum and how it is approached and discussed.

Focus on relationships rather than on the completion of the intended agenda. Allow discussion to go where it needs to go, according to the needs of the group.

We have found that smaller groups (with 3-6 participants) provide the best environment for spiritual growth. Small groups are how Christians experience *koinonia* (intimate, supportive fellowship), and walk together and support each other in their faith journeys. The Christian Church needs both expressions of church as described in the Acts 2 community: gathering for worship in the temple (large group) as well as gathering in homes for the breaking of the bread (Acts 2:46). For congregations that want to grow in faith, spirit, and mission, small groups will need to become an essential part of the congregational structure, not just an additional activity for those who like to participate in small groups.

Small groups will typically have these components: time for prayer, time to share how life is going (and support of each other), time for Bible study, and time for discussion of the weekly chapter.

Small groups have been the environment in which many people of Peace Lutheran have learned to pray aloud with each other. We learn to pray with others by practicing praying with and for others. Consider a variety of prayer methods to encourage growth in prayer (read prayers, written prayers, circle prayers, sentence prayers, spontaneous prayer, prayer journals, among many other methods.[105]

A small group covenant helps a group agree to expectations and accountability. (See below for suggestions.)

Everyone in the group should be encouraged to share, but should not be pressured to do so. There is no need for each person to provide his or her answers to each question that is discussed. The group should learn not to rush to fill in the silences.

People will have different perspectives, experiences, and interpretations of the Bible.

Group members should agree not to attempt to give advice or fix one another's problems, unless asked for help. This is not a therapy group.

The use of "I statements" (rather than "you," "we," or "they") helps participants to avoid speaking for or about others.

Groups need to decide when and if new members are to be welcomed into the group.

Confidentiality is essential for a group to have a foundation of honesty and to build trust.

The group should agree to a shared leadership unless one person is appointed as the convener. In this case, the convener can lead and model leadership of the weekly meeting for a few weeks until the group is ready to share and rotate the leadership.

A Small Group Covenant

A small group covenant can be a helpful way of clarifying the group's expectations as well as building the group's accountability. A covenant should include agreement to these kinds of commitments:

> completion of the weekly assignment;
>
> participation in the weekly group gathering;
>
> maintaining an environment of honesty, trust, and confidentiality;
>
> daily time with God;
>
> prayer for each other during the week.

A sample small group covenant follows. The small group should agree to the meeting schedule and any logistics.

A Sample Small Group Covenant[106]

Purpose of the group: In order to grow in Christ, walk together, and support each other, we give ourselves to this small group opportunity, praying that the Holy Spirit will use it and grow us for God's purpose.

We agree to these commitments:

- to read and complete the weekly assignment;
- to regularly participate in the weekly group gathering;
- to maintain an environment of honesty, trust, and confidentiality;
- to spend daily time with God;
- to pray for each other during the week.

Our small group will meet weekly according to this schedule:

Our small group will exist together for this intended length of time:

_____ten to twelve weeks.

_____ten weeks, and then perhaps another ten weeks…

_____one year

Signed: _____

Names and phone numbers/email addresses of group members

Discipleship Groups of 3 and 4

In 2004, Peace Lutheran Church, Charlottesville, Virginia, began its first discipleship group of four men. Although related to the developing mission of the congregation, it did not really arise from an intentional implementation of a vision or mission objective. In a search for small group resources, I came across Greg Ogden's book, *Transforming Discipleship*, and his long term approach to spiritual growth in the congregation was an intriguing concept. I came to agree with Ogden's conclusion that discipleship groups of 3-4 persons are the optimal size for the discipling process.[107]

Ogden argues that small groups of three or four people provide the best environment for discipling people in the faith; small groups of three or four people best provide the three essential ingredients for transformation: the Word of God (the appropriation of scriptural truth), transparent, trusting relationships ("the extent to which we are willing to reveal to others those areas of our life that need God's transforming touch is the extent to which we are inviting the Holy Spirit to make us new"), and mutual accountability (encouraging and holding each other accountable to the discipleship covenant to which they have agreed).[108]

To clarify, a small group of 3-4 persons will have an advantage over a larger group of 6-10 people, in that self-disclosure and openness become "increasingly difficult in direct proportion to the size of the group," and "greater numbers decrease access to a person's life."[109] In other words, the larger the group, the more likely one can hide, in terms of group discussion, sharing one's life, and fulfilling the covenant. When a group has only three or four persons, full participation by all is both necessary and obvious. The fact that most discipleship groups meet together for at least a year helps to develop the transparent trust and accountability, and over the course of a year group members will give and receive the care of Christ though life's highs and lows. The group members will be able to support and care for one another through the natural rhythm of periods of grief and difficulty as well as joys and celebrations ("If one member suffers, all suffer together with it; if one member is honored, all rejoice together with it" 1 Corinthians 12:26).

Discipleship groups at Peace Lutheran Church have been groups of 3-4 persons (either men's or women's groups) which typically meet together weekly, for at least 90 minutes, for prayer, discussion about the biblical readings and workbook questions, and fellowship and care for each other. The convener calls the group together and models the leadership for a few sessions, and then the group rotates with a shared leadership. All share an equal responsibility, and no one person is the "teacher."

Discipleship groups have been a most significant step in developing a congregational culture of discipleship. Discipleship groups have become stepping stones into other faith-forming experiences (small groups, Bible studies, retreats, and mission trips) which invite people to step out of their comfort zones and to place themselves into new contexts which invite them to be open to God and to other people. What has been experienced by the people of Peace is that God uses this stepping into a new experience as a way to bring about spiritual growth.

Endnotes

[1]John D. Herman, *Growing Disciples: The Impact of Discipleship Groups on the Spiritual Vitality of a Congregation*, 2. Thesis (D. Min.)—The Lutheran Theological Seminary at Philadelphia, 2011.

[2]The "baptismal covenant" language and services of Affirmation of Baptism can also be found in the Presbyterian tradition (*Book of Common Worship*, 403-484), in the Episcopalian tradition (*Book of Common Prayer*, 304-305) and in the United Methodist tradition (http://www.umc.org/site/c.lwL4KnN1LtH/b.1697379/k.9027/Baptism_Overview.htm).

[3]Evangelical Lutheran Church in America and Evangelical Lutheran Church in Canada, *Evangelical Lutheran Worship*. (Minneapolis, MN: Augsburg Fortress, 2006), 97.

[4]Ibid., 228.

[5] Glenn McDonald, *Living Beyond the Sanctuary*. (Grand Haven, Mich: Faith Walk Pub, 2008), 11.

[6]Ogden, *Discipleship Essentials*, 24.

[7]Herman, *Growing Disciples, 2.*

[8]Ogden, *Discipleship Essentials*, 21.

[9]Dave Daubert and Tana Kjos. *Reclaiming the "V" Word: Renewing Life at Its Vocational Core*. (Minneapolis, MN: Augsburg Fortress, 2009), 19.

[10]Adapted from Greg Ogden, *Transforming Discipleship*, 77.

[11]LIFEKEYS is a spiritually-based comprehensive program for discovering your life gifts, spiritual gifts, personality type, values and passions.

[12]Lee C. Camp, *Mere Discipleship: Radical Christianity in a Rebellious World*. (Grand Rapids: Brazos Press, 2003), 177.

[13]Michael W. Foss, *Power Surge: Six Marks of Discipleship for a Changing Church*. (Minneapolis: Fortress Press, 2000), 102.

[14]Ibid., 73.

[15]Ibid.

[16]*ELW*, 72.

[17]Richard Foster, *Life With God: Reading the Bible for Spiritual Transformation*. (New York: HarperCollins, 2010), 10-13.

[18]Frederick Buechner, *Peculiar Treasures: A Biblical Who's Who*. (San Francisco: Harper & Row, 1979), 115.

[19]Diane L. Jacobson and Mark Allan Powell. *Opening the Book of Faith: Lutheran Insights for Bible Study*. (Minneapolis, MN: Augsburg Fortress, 2008) 31

[20]Ibid., 32.

[21]Ibid., 33.

[22]Kierkegaard, *Provocations: Spiritual Writings of Kierkegaard*, ed. Charles E. Moore (Farmington, PA: Plough, 2002), 201.

[23]Foss, *Power Surge*, 94-95.

[24]Marjorie J. Thompson, *Soul Feast: An Invitation to the Christian Spiritual Life*. (Louisville, KY: Westminster John Knox Press, 1995), 58-59.

[25]John P. Bowen, *Evangelism for "Normal" People: Good News for Those Looking for a Fresh Approach*. (Minneapolis: Augsburg Fortress, 2002), 90.

[26]Philip D. Kenneson, *Life on the Vine: Cultivating the Fruit of the Spirit in Christian Community*. (Downers Grove, IL: InterVarsity Press, 1999), 48.

[27]Darlene Zschech, *Extravagant Worship*. (Minneapolis, MN: Bethany House, 2002), 27.

[28]Ibid.

[29]*ELW*, 108.

[30]*ELW*: Narrative Holy Communion, 6.

[31]*ELW*, 111.

[32]R.E. Lybrand, *Holy Communion Is...:Thirteen Communion Messages.* (Lima, OH: CSS Publishing, 1987), 18.

[33]Evangelical Lutheran Church in America, and Evangelical Lutheran Church in Canada. *Evangelical Lutheran Worship: Leaders Desk Edition.* (Minneapolis: Augsburg Fortress, 2006), 200.

[34]Martin Luther, *Large Catechism: The Sacrament of the Altar,* 24-25, in Robert Kolb, Timothy J. Wengert, and Charles P. Arand. *The Book of Concord: The Confessions of the Evangelical Lutheran Church.* (Minneapolis: Fortress Press, 2000).

[35]*ELW*: Narrative Holy Communion, 7.

[36]Ibid., 8.

[37]*ELW*, 114.

[38]*ELW*, 72.

[39]This is one of the six marks of discipleship painted on the sanctuary walls at Peace Lutheran Church, Charlottesville, VA (adapted from Glenn McDonald, *The Disciple Making Church*).

[40]Kelly A. Fryer, *Reclaiming the "E" Word: Waking Up to Our Evangelical Identity.* (Minneapolis: Augsburg Fortress, 2008), 7.

[41]Ibid., 8.

[42]Michael W. Foss, *From Members to Disciples: Leadership Lessons from the Book of Acts.* (Nashville: Abingdon Press, 2007), 51.

[43]Ibid., 56.

[44]*Transformation Journal: a one year road trip with Jesus. Part Two: Jesus and Servanthood.* (Ginghamsburg Church, 2003).

[45]This is Lore Amlinger's translation of a prayer from John Henry Newman from a German devotional, *Die Lusungen*-2008.

[46]Richard J. Foster, *Celebration of Discipline: The Path to Spiritual Growth.* (San Francisco: Harper & Row, 1978, 126.

[47]Ibid., 126-27.

[48]Ibid., 130.

[49]*Transformation Journal: Jesus and Servanthood.*

[50]Shane Claiborne, *The Irresistible Revolution: Living As an Ordinary Radical.* (Grand Rapids, MI: Zondervan, 2006), 78.

[51]Ibid., 132.

[52] Bonhoeffer, Dietrich; Albrecht Schonherr; Geffrey B. Kelly; Daniel W. Bloesch (2010-08-18). *Life Together and Prayerbook of the Bible* (Dietrich Bonhoeffer Works): Life Together and Prayer Book of the Bible v. 5 (pp. 99-100). Augsburg Fortress Publishers. Kindle Edition.

[53]Foster, *Celebration of Discipline*, 140.

[54]J.R.R. Tolkien, *The Hobbit, or, There and Back Again.* (Boston: Houghton Mifflin, 1966), 18.

[55]Jim Wallis, *Faith Works: How to Live Your Beliefs and Ignite Positive Social Change.* (New York: Random house, 2000), 35.

[56]Ibid.

[57]Ibid., 36.

[58]Ibid., 42.

[59]Ibid.

[60]Ibid.

[61]Claiborne, 128-29.

[62]Wallis, *Faith Works*, 43.

[63]*ELW*, 79.

[64]Bonhoeffer, Dietrich; Albrecht Schonherr; Geffrey B. Kelly; Daniel W. Bloesch (2010-08-18). *Life Together and Prayerbook of the Bible* (Dietrich Bonhoeffer Works): Life Together and Prayer Book of the Bible v. 5 (p. 100). Augsburg Fortress Publishers. Kindle Edition.

[65]Daniel Erlander, *Baptized, We Live: Lutheranism As a Way of Life.* (Chelan, WA: Holden Village, 1981), 26.

[66]*ELW*, 79.

[67]Philip Yancey, *The Jesus I Never Knew,* (Grand Rapids, MI: Zondervan, 1995), 39.

[68]Claiborne, 129.

[69]Erlander, 26. Duchrow suggests the prisoners are in prison above all because of debt. See Ulrich Duchrow and Elizabeth Hicks, *Alternatives to Global Capitalism: Drawn from Biblical History, Design for Political Action.* (Utrecht: International Books, 1995), 204.

[70]Lowell O. Erdahl, *Pro-Life/Pro-Peace: Life-Affirming Alternatives to Abortion, War, Mercy Killing, and the Death Penalty.* (Minneapolis: Augsburg Pub. House, 1986), 68.

[71]Archbishop Oscar Romero, sermon, 2/5/78.

[72]Ronald J. Sider, *Rich Christians in an Age of Hunger: A Biblical Study.* (Downers Grove, IL: Intervarsity Press, 1977), 1.

[73]Mars Hill. Narrative Theology. http://marshill.org/believe/about/narrative-theology/ (accessed 12/12/11)

[74]*ELW,* 79.

[75]John F. Kavanaugh, *Following Christ in a Consumer Society: The Spirituality of Cultural Resistance.* (Maryknoll, NY: Orbis Books, 1981), 91.

[76]Walter Brueggemann, Sharon Daloz Parks, and Thomas H. Groome. *To Act Justly, Love Tenderly, Walk Humbly: An Agenda for Ministers.* (New York: Paulist Press, 1986), 55.

[77]*ELW*, 79.

[78]Claiborne, 149.

[79]Johann Christoph Arnold, *Seeking Peace: Notes and Conversations Along the Way.* (Farmington, PA: Plough Pub. House, 1998), 3.

[80]Ibid., 13.

[81]Spangler, Ann (2009-07-20). *Praying the Names of Jesus: A Daily Guide* (pp. 107-108). Zondervan. Kindle Edition.

[82]Ibid., 108.

[83]Philip H. Pfatteicher and Carlos R. Messerli. *Manual on the Liturgy: Lutheran Book of Worship.* (Minneapolis: Augsburg Pub. House, 1978), 226.

[84]*ELW*, 76.

[85]Sider, *Rich Christians in An Age of Hunger*, 209-210.

[86]*Evangelical Lutheran Worship*, 75.

[87]*ELW*, 76.

[88]Ibid., 80.

[89]*Evangelical Lutheran Worship*, 237.

[90]Yancey, *The Jesus I Never Knew*, 25.

[91]Foster, *Life With God*, 15-16.

[92]Marcus Borg, *The Heart of Christianity: Rediscovering a Life of Faith.* (San Francisco: HarperSanFrancisco, 2003), 187.

[93]Ibid., 189.

[94]McDonald, *The Disciple Making Church.*

[95]Foster, *Celebration of Discipline*, 7.

[96]Glenn McDonald, *Living Beyond the Sanctuary*, 20.

[97]Foss, *Power Surge*, 106.

[98]McDonald, *The Disciple Making Church*, 128.

[99]Ibid., 155.

[100]Ibid., 169.

[101]Ibid., 185, 197.

[102]Ibid., 211.

[103]Foster, *Life With God*, 17.

[104]Affirmation of Baptism, text reprinted from *Evangelical Lutheran Worship* pages 234-237 Copyright 2006 Evangelical Lutheran Church in America, published by Augsburg Fortress

[105]For guidance in developing prayer, see "Prayer in small groups" in Augsburg Fortress (Publisher), *Starting Small Groups—and Keeping Them Going.* (Minneapolis, Augsburg Fortress, 1995), 120.

[106]Sample small group covenants can be found in Greg Ogden, *Discipleship Essentials: A Guide to Building Your Life in Christ.* (Downers Grove, IL: IVP Connect, 2007), 14, and in *Starting Small Groups—and Keeping Them Going,* 121.

[107]Greg Ogden, *Transforming Discipleship: Making Disciples a Few at a Time.* (Downers Grove, IL: InterVarsity, 2003), 171-72.

[108]Greg Ogden, *Making Disciples Jesus' Way: A Few At A Time,* 2007. http://www.gregogden.com/PDFs/ TransformingDiscipleshipSummary.pdf (accessed 9/20/10).

[109]Greg Ogden, *Discipleship Essentials,* 11.